THE BUSLIFE KITCHEN

CUISINE FOR THE MODERN NOMAD

A. J. FORGET

COVER ART BY PHILIPPE WILLIS

First paperback edition September 2022
Printed in PRC

Photography by A. J. Forget, Ayana Otteman, & Dan Gleason
Cover Art by Philippe Willis

ISBN 979-8-9857083-0-1 (paperback)
ISBN 979-8-9857083-1-8 (ebook)

www.thebuslifekitchen.com

For Ayana,
the only person I could love sharing
90 square feet with

TABLE OF CONTENTS

INTRODUCTION

Take a look at that picture at the bottom of the page. That's our house. That little bus, all 90 square feet of it, is where this cookbook was developed. When it comes to cooking really good food, a tiny kitchen like ours might seem like a hindrance, an obstacle, or a plainly insurmountable problem, but after cooking in a miniscule kitchen for some time now, I am here to tell you that it is a boon. Cooking in a kitchen with a tiny counter, limited tools, and no hot water certainly doesn't make the job any easier, but it does make you better. In a kitchen like that, there's no room to be lazy or sloppy. There are no extra ingredients in the fridge if you make a mistake, and no extra space on the counter if you realize you forgot to prepare a part of your mise en place. A tiny kitchen trains you to be more aware, mindful, and efficient. It may be challenging now, but this cookbook is here to help with that. And, once you get used to dishing up gourmet fare from your rig, the next time you are at someone else's house, with big, wide counters and unlimited hot water, it'll be a breeze.

I know that for many buslifers, vanlifers, RV folks, tiny-house-dwellers, car campers, and other cramped kitchen owners, the focus is usually on fast, easy, and often boring food. Most meals are planned around fueling the body for adventure, keeping costs down, and not dirtying too many dishes. If that's how you eat, that's great, and there are plenty of tasty and quick recipes in here. But that is not how we eat. I believe that meals are an event to be savored. Perhaps not all of them, we all need simple breakfasts and quiet lunches most days, but I believe that at least one meal a

day should be a shared experience. I'm sure you already have everything you need to class up a couple boxes of mac and cheese after a long day on the trail, but what about when you want to invite the neighbors over to your van for a feast? That's where these recipes come in.

In this book is what I call "cuisine for the modern nomad," a plethora of delicious dishes spanning many cuisines and varying in complexity from simple weeknight fare to exotic, feast-worthy delights. There are over 100 recipes, from over 15 cuisines, everything from chilaquiles and poke

bowls to eggs benedict and crème brûlée—there's even a recipe for a roast turkey. And, best of all, every single one of them can be cooked on the stovetop—no oven needed.

I have spent years exploring these cuisines, perfecting these recipes, and making them all simple and accessible to cook no matter how small or basic your kitchen. With a few pots and pans, a couple of tools, and a pinch of gumption, anyone can whip up a michelin-star-worthy feast. And, when I say anyone, I mean you, dear reader. So, sharpen up those knives, crack a beer, and make friends with your neighbors, because you are about to cook up some meals that are too good not to share.

ITALIAN RECIPES

THREE PEPPER BRUSCHETTA

Bruschetta (pronounced brew-sket-uh) is not the same dish in the old country that it is here in the states. The chopped tomato appetizer that we think of as bruschetta is actually one of many varieties. At its base, bruschetta is simply a dish of grilled bread, rubbed with garlic and brushed with olive oil. The dish gets its name from the latin word, bruscare, which means to grill. With grilled bread at the base, just about anything you put on top can be called bruschetta.

This recipe is adapted from a dish served at our favorite Italian restaurant in Boulder, which is no longer in operation. They used to have the best happy hour in town. And, when they first opened, this bruschetta dish was large enough for the two of us to split one for supper. Alas, they did not survive the first round of pandemic shutdowns. But, fortunately for all of us, I figured out how to make this recipe at home months before they shut their doors for good.

INGREDIENTS:

1 red bell pepper
1 yellow/orange bell pepper
1 green bell pepper
1 cup ricotta
1 clove garlic
1 lemon
Good, crusty bread
Salt, to taste

DIRECTIONS:

Roast the peppers. You can do this directly over a burner, on a campfire, or under a broiler. You want them nicely blistered, and a bit of char doesn't hurt anything. Once cooled, remove the skins and as much of the interior fibers and seeds as you can.

Slice the roasted peppers thinly, and salt them to taste. They can be served immediately or made ahead and stored in a jar or covered bowl in the fridge for a few days.

To serve, toast or grill the bread slices and rub them with a clove of garlic that has been split in half. Drape a few slices of roasted pepper over a good smear of ricotta on the toasts. Squeeze a bit of lemon over the top and add a sprinkle more salt, if desired.

Vodka sauce, at the foundation, is just a tomato and cream sauce laced with a bit of red pepper and a splash of vodka. The liquor may have initially been added to the sauce as a marketing ploy by distillers, but it does serve a purpose: at low concentrations, alcohol increases the perception of aroma, so the splash of vodka bumps that flavor meter up a notch. Additionally, the alcohol serves as an emulsifier, helping to keep the mixture of tomato and cream silky smooth.

INGREDIENTS:

1 lb. rigatoni or penne
1 large shallot, finely chopped
4 cloves garlic, minced
4 oz. parmesan, grated
3 tbsp olive oil
1 4.5 oz. tube of double-concentrated tomato paste
½ tsp crushed red pepper
¼ tsp black pepper
2 oz. vodka
¾ cup heavy cream
Basil, to garnish

DIRECTIONS:

Start the water for the pasta in a large pot and add a liberal quantity of salt. Once boiling, toss the rigatoni in. While the pasta cooks, start work on the sauce.

Add olive oil to another large pot over medium heat. Add the shallots and garlic to the pan along with a bit of oil. Cook them until they are browning at the edges, 5 or 6 minutes. Then add the tomato paste and red pepper. Cook this until the paste darkens slightly and sticks to the bottom.

Deglaze the pan with the vodka. Be sure to scrape the bottom of any dark burned bits. As this is boiling, scoop out ¼ cup of the pasta water and add ¾ cup heavy cream. The pasta water brings the cream up to temperature so that it will not scald when added to the hot pan.

Reduce heat to low and slowly stir the cream mixture in. Then add half the grated parmesan while stirring, allowing it to melt into the mix. Add another half cup of pasta water a bit at a time while stirring. This thins the sauce. If you'd like the sauce thinner, you can continue slowly adding pasta water. Add the drained pasta and stir to coat well.

Serve the pasta topped with the remaining parmesan cheese, a few cranks of black pepper, and a bit of chopped fresh basil.

CHICKEN PICCATA

Piccata is a classic dish in both Italian and Italian-American cuisine, though the term piccata actually refers to a method of preparation rather than a dish itself. In the US, the most commonly used protein in this dish is chicken, in Italy it is typically made with veal, but everywhere the preparation is the same: the protein is pounded thin, dredged in flour, fried in oil, and served with a lemon, caper, and butter sauce. There are a few steps to it, but after you've cooked it once, it is all simple enough to be done without a recipe, and is so delicious it will definitely end up in your list of fancy weeknight meals.

INGREDIENTS:

2 chicken breasts, sliced in half and pounded thin
Flour
¼ cup olive oil
2 tbsp butter
Juice of 1 lemon
¼ cup sherry or dry white wine
½ cup chicken broth
¼ cup capers, drained
4 cloves garlic, minced
2 tbsp chopped parsley

DIRECTIONS:

Cut the chicken breasts in half and pound thin. This can be done between two pieces of plastic wrap to reduce the mess. I typically use my fist for pounding, but a meat mallet or wine bottle will also do (just be careful with glass).

Season the cutlets with salt and pepper, then dredge in flour and fry in 1/4 cup olive oil over medium-high heat until well browned on both sides, a few minutes each. Remove the chicken to a plate to drain and reduce the heat to medium.

Add the garlic and allow it to cook for 30-60 seconds. As soon as it begins to brown, add the capers and wine. Scrape the bottom of the pan to get up any fond.

Add the chicken broth and cook for 30 seconds. Add 2 tbsp butter and whisk as it melts to incorporate it. Return the chicken to the pan and allow it to cook for around 2 minutes, then remove it to a plate.

Increase heat to medium-high and cook the sauce around one additional minute to allow it to reduce further.

Remove from heat. Add lemon juice and whisk to mix well. Add salt to taste. Serve one cutlet per person with a generous amount of sauce.

This is the most popular and recognizable bruschetta in the states: the familiar dish of chopped tomato and basil. While it may not be the most exciting option, there is a reason that this appetizer is such a classic. It is light, it is refreshing, and it absolutely screams summer. While it is delicious at any time of year, this dish is especially delightful if you happen to have a few nice, ripe tomatoes fresh from the garden.

INGREDIENTS:

1 ½ lbs. roma tomatoes, seeded (~5 tomatoes)
2 large cloves garlic, minced
1 tbsp olive oil
1 tsp balsamic vinegar
6-8 basil leaves, chiffonade
¾ tsp salt
½ tsp pepper

DIRECTIONS:

Seed the tomatoes and chop them to a large dice. Add minced garlic, finely chopped basil, olive oil, balsamic vinegar, salt, and pepper, and mix well. Place this in the refrigerator for at least an hour before serving to allow the flavors to meld.

Serve a dollop on good grilled bread slices brushed with olive oil and sprinkled with salt.

FENNEL AND ORANGE SALAD

Fennel and orange are both cool-weather crops grown in southern Italy, making this salad perfect for the moderate temperatures of a buslife winter spent following the good weather southward.

The mild flavors of fennel and cucumber are spiked with bursts of red onion and orange to create a truly elegant salad. A bed of lightly dressed arugula adds a peppery kick and stretches those flavors into a dish large enough for the whole family, while a sprinkling of pomegranate pips adds color and another tangy burst of flavor, and a few shavings of salty parmesan balances the sweetness of the fruits. It is a truly magnificent salad for the autumn and winter months.

INGREDIENTS:

2 Fennel bulbs, shaved
1 Cucumber, peeled and thinly slices
3 Oranges, peeled and thinly sliced
½ small Red Onion, shaved
3 tbsp Mint, coarsely chopped
6 cups Baby Arugula
2 tbsp Olive Oil
1 tbsp White Wine Vinegar
Salt + Pepper
Parmesan Cheese, shaved
¼-½ cup pomegranate pips

DIRECTIONS:

This recipe is a great time to break out the mandolin if you have one, as thin slicing is the name of the game here. If not, that's okay, it is just a bit more knife work.

Peel the oranges and slice them into thin discs using a sharp knife. Slices should be around ¼" thick.

Do the same with the cucumber, but feel free to use the mandolin here, if you have one. Slices should be ⅛"-¼" thick.

Shave the fennel and red onion to roughly ⅛" thick slices.

Add the baby arugula to a large salad bowl and dress with olive oil and white wine vinegar. Add salt and pepper to taste and toss to cover.

On each plate, place a bed of the dressed arugula. Cover the arugula with a layer of cucumber, fennel, and red onion. Place orange slices overtop. Sprinkle with pomegranate pips, coarsely chopped mint, and shaved parmesan. Either that, or do it all in one big bowl and let people sort it out for themselves.

SPAGHETTI CARBONARA

Spaghetti carbonara is a dish made with pasta, cured pork, cheese, and eggs. The raw eggs and cheese are combined with a bit of pasta water to create a silky smooth and absolutely delicious sauce. Interestingly, while it does resemble the classic dish pasta alla gricia, carbonara is not mentioned before World War II. It is thought to have first come about after the American military ousted Axis forces in Italy, and were supplying the people of Rome with rations containing a great deal of bacon and powdered eggs. Italians do not typically indulge in large breakfasts, so these ingredients naturally found their way into pasta, creating spaghetti carbonara.

INGREDIENTS:

1 lb. spaghetti
1 cup freshly grated parmesan cheese
¼ lb. bacon
4 egg yolks
2 eggs
Salt + Pepper

DIRECTIONS:

Begin by cooking your pasta in well-salted water. The pasta water is an important part of this dish, so season it well. Around 1-2 tbsps per pound of pasta (~4 quarts of water) is reasonable. The water should taste like the sea.

In another pot, fry your bacon pieces until nicely crispy. Remove them to a plate to drain, and remove the pan from heat.

Beat the eggs and yolks in a small bowl and add the cup of grated parmesan as well as ¼ tsp freshly ground black pepper. Set aside for now.

Turn off the heat on the pasta once it is cooked al dente and remove the pasta from the pot, while reserving the pasta water. Add the pasta to the pan used to cook the bacon and cook over medium heat until the water is mostly cooked off. Remove from heat.

Whisk ¼ cup of the pasta water into your egg and cheese mixture to temper it. Pour this over the pasta slowly, in batches, while stirring. It should make a beautiful creamy sauce. If your sauce is too thick, you can further thin it with additional pasta water.

Garnish with parmesan cheese, crispy bacon, and fresh black pepper.

Spaghetti carbonara is typically made with cured pork, but this vegetarian recipe creates that same depth of flavor using smoked paprika. The smokiness that is often lost in carbonara really shines in this dish, complemented by a bit of sweetness from onions and bell pepper. It is not traditional, and might drive some Italian folks to pull their hair out, but it is damn delicious.

INGREDIENTS:

1 lb. Spaghetti
¼ cup red bell pepper, finely diced
2 cloves garlic, minced
1 medium yellow onion, finely diced
¼ cup olive oil
4 egg yolks
2 eggs
1 cup freshly grated parmesan cheese
1 tsp smoked paprika
¼ tsp freshly ground black pepper
Salt, to taste

DIRECTIONS:

In one pot, boil your spaghetti in well-salted water until al dente. In another pot, saute the red bell pepper, garlic, and onion in ¼ cup good olive oil. When fragrant and mostly softened, turn off heat.

Beat the eggs and yolks and add the cup of grated parmesan as well as the smoked paprika and black pepper. Set aside for now.

Drain the pasta, reserving the pasta water.

Add the pasta to the pot with the vegetables and cook over medium heat until the water is mostly cooked off. Remove from heat.

Whisk ¼ cup of the pasta water into your egg and cheese mixture to temper it. Pour this over the pasta slowly, in batches, while stirring. It should make a beautiful creamy sauce. If the egg in the sauce cooks, your pasta is too hot, allow it to cool more before adding the sauce. If your sauce is too thick, you can further thin it with the reserved pasta water.

Garnish with additional parmesan cheese, smoked paprika, black pepper, finely chopped parsley, and additional salt, if desired.

ITALIAN-STYLE GREENS

This method of cooking greens was historically used throughout the Mediterranean region, often with whatever greens could be foraged locally at the time. While the exact ingredients may have varied throughout the year and from place to place, a dish of cooked greens with plenty of olive oil and some garlic for flavor is about as healthy and delicious as it gets. I use this method to cook spinach, kale, and any wild greens that I forage myself. It is always fantastic.

INGREDIENTS:

4 cups greens of choice, chopped into 2" pieces
3 cloves garlic, smashed
¼ cup olive oil
½ tsp crushed red pepper
Salt, to taste
Lemon Juice, to taste

DIRECTIONS:

Blanch your washed and chopped greens in salted water until tender, around ten minutes. Once cooked, drain the greens in a colander. Press out the excess moisture.

This first step can be done well ahead. If you have a bag of spinach in the fridge that is nearing its expiration, give it a blanch now and finish the cooking later, when you are ready to eat it.

Once the greens are cooked and drained, start a skillet over medium heat and add your olive oil. Once it is hot, add the garlic and crushed red pepper. Cook these until the aroma is excellent, but be sure you do not burn the garlic. Add the cooked and drained greens to the pan and sauté until well mixed and heated through, just a minute or two. Add salt and pepper to taste.

Remove the greens to a plate and finish with a squeeze of lemon juice.

MEXICAN RECIPES

ELOTES

In reality, elote translates to corn on the cob, but it has also come to mean grilled corn slathered in a tangy, spicy sauce and sprinkled with salty cheese. This dish is also referred to as Mexican street corn, as it is a popular food stall dish. Whatever you call it, it's a really easy side to throw together for a taco night or barbecue, and it is damn good.

I suggest shucking the corn before grilling to create a bit of char on the kernels. As for the sauce, some folks use all mayo, but I prefer a sauce dominated by sour cream. Make the sauce early in the day so the flavors have time to meld.

INGREDIENTS:

Corn:
3 ears of corn
1 tbsp oil
Salt

Sauce:
¼ cup mayonnaise
½ cup sour cream
Juice of 1 lime
1 tsp chipotle powder
1 tsp garlic powder
1 tsp cumin

Garnish:
¼ cup Queso Fresco
Cilantro, finely chopped

DIRECTIONS:

Make the sauce at least a few hours in advance to allow the flavors to meld. Simply mix the mayonnaise, sour cream, lime juice, and spices in a small bowl and store in the refrigerator.

Lightly coat the corn with oil, sprinkle with salt, and grill over a medium-high heat grill or grill pan until kernels are tender and it is lightly charred on all sides. Remove from heat and allow to cool for a few minutes.

To serve, add the sauce liberally and garnish with a heavy sprinkle of crumbled cheese and cilantro.

SALSA ROJA

A good salsa roja recipe is something we should have in our back pocket. There are an unlimited number of ways to make salsa, and I am all about exploration and creativity, but for me no salsa platter is complete without a basic, perfect salsa roja. This is the foundation from which you branch out to something like a mango habanero or a creamy avocado. All of those salsa variations are delicious, but after each chip dipped in one of those experiments, I find myself coming back to the good old salsa roja to reset the palate.

I also like this recipe because, frankly, I hate buying salsa in a jar. Not only is jar salsa expensive and the quality low, it also adds a glass jar to our perpetually too-full trash can (one of those buslife resources that we are constantly trying to manage). And with a recipe this simple, there is really no reason to buy jar salsa again. It's cheaper, it's tastier, and it doesn't create another piece of garbage—can't beat that.

INGREDIENTS:

5 roma tomatoes, seeded
1 cup white onion
½ cup cilantro, loosely packed
2 jalapenos (seeded if you are sensitive to heat)
2 cloves garlic
1 tsp cumin
Juice from 1 lime
¼ cup water
Salt, to taste

DIRECTIONS:

Begin by seeding the roma tomatoes. Coarsely chop the remaining ingredients and toss it all in the food processor. If you are sensitive to heat, be sure to remove the seeds from the chiles.

Blend in the food processor until the desired consistency is reached. You can leave it a bit chunky, if that is how you like your salsa—I like it well-blended.

Taste, and add additional salt or lime if desired.

Serve with lots of chips and some good, cold, Mexican lagers.

There are a lot of delicious peppers out there, but for me poblanos are unrivaled. Unfortunately, it can be really difficult to get that amazing flavor to come through in a meal. It is a delicate aroma which is easily destroyed or overpowered. A whole bunch of peppers added to a dish sometimes leads to nothing more than an extra bit of green. Thankfully, in rajas con crema there is a solution. This dish manages to capture that delicate, elusive flavor and let it truly dance across your palate.

INGREDIENTS:

8 poblano peppers
1 small white onion
1 cup mexican crema
½ cup monterey jack
1 tsp chili powder
Salt, to taste

DIRECTIONS:

Char the outside of the poblanos. You can do this over the burner of a gas stove, on the grill, or under a broiler. You want them to be very blistered, and char doesn't hurt anything. Do this first, and then set them aside to cool a while.

Once the chiles are cool enough to touch, peel off the skin. Do your best to get it all, and then slice off the stems and any internal fibers remaining. Scoop out as many of the seeds as you can.

When your chiles are all peeled, slice them into ¼" to ½" strips lengthwise. Then slice these strips down to around 3" in length. Slice your onion into quarters and then slice the quarters in strips to match the chiles. Heat 1 tbsp of oil in a pan over medium-high heat and, when hot, add the onion. Cook for around 5 minutes, until lightly browned.

Reduce the heat to medium-low, add the peppers and crema, and allow to simmer for another 4-5 minutes. If you cannot find mexican crema where you are, you can use a combination of milk and sour cream. Crema tastes like cream, it doesn't have the soured aspect, but is somewhere between whipping cream and sour cream in terms of consistency.

After the peppers, onions, and crema have had a chance to meld together a bit, add your cheese and chili powder. The cheese should quickly melt and slightly thicken the sauce. Add salt to taste now as well.

Serve with warm corn tortillas, cilantro, diced onion, and spicy hot sauce.

THE BEST GUACAMOLE YOU'VE EVER HAD

I would guess that just about everyone reading this recipe has made guacamole before. It is difficult to mess up: mash up some avocados with onions, maybe aldd some garlic and tomatoes, a touch of lime and salt, and you're there. Simple and wonderful. But what if I told you there was a better way? I know, I know, it's hard to have your whole guac-iverse turned upside down like this, and I was reluctant at first, but one chip and you'll be a believer.

The trick to the best guacamole you've ever had lies in the food processor. By creating a paste from the onion, cilantro, chilies, and garlic, you allow those ingredients to truly permeate the dish, so each bite sings with the flavors of not only avocado and salt, but also spicy chilies, herbal cilantro, and bright lime.

INGREDIENTS:

3 extra large avocados (or 5 medium)
¼ cup white onion
1 serrano pepper
2 jalapeno peppers
3 tbsp cilantro
1 clove garlic
Juice of 1 lime
¼ cup roma tomato, finely chopped
1 tsp cumin
Salt, to taste

DIRECTIONS:

Add cilantro, lime juice, garlic, jalapeno, serranos, and all but 1 tbsp of the onion to a food processor. Blend until a paste is formed. If you are sensitive to heat, remove the seeds from your chiles before doing this—these peppers give the guacamole a nice kick.

In a large bowl, combine the paste from the food processor with the peeled and pitted avocados. Toss in all but 1 tbsp of the finely chopped roma tomatoes as well. Add the cumin and a bit of salt now. Mash this all together until your desired consistency is reached. Guacamole should, ideally, still have some texture to it, it is not meant to be a puree. Taste, and add more salt, lime, or cumin as necessary.

To serve, top with the reserved finely chopped onion, tomato, and cilantro, and accompany with tortilla chips and probably a few cold lagers.

The weeks spent perfecting chicken tinga were undoubtedly some of the best of my life. Not only were we eating amazing tacos every few days, but our friends also kept dropping in for dinner. Once you've tasted these tacos, it is not hard to see why. Chicken tinga is made by simmering chicken thighs in broth, tomato, and chipotle until easily shredded. Further depth is added to the sauce with the right amount of spice, alliums, acids, and just a touch of sugar. The final product is a perfect filling for tacos or burritos, or simply a delicious meat to serve beside rice and beans.

INGREDIENTS:

2 lbs. boneless, skinless chicken thighs
4 cloves garlic, minced
1 medium white onion, quartered and sliced in ½" slices
3 oz. tomato paste
½ cup chipotles in adobo, minced
1 tsp cumin
2 tbsp cider vinegar
1 cup chicken broth
1 tbsp + 1 tsp sugar
Salt
Half of 1 lime

DIRECTIONS:

Heat 1 tbsp of oil in a heavy-bottomed pot with a lid over medium-high heat. Add the chicken and onions and cook for 5-10 minutes to get a bit of browning.

When the meat is browned, reduce the heat to medium and add the garlic and tomato paste. Mix around well and cook for 3-5 minutes to darken the tomato paste. Then add the chipotles in adobo (seeded if you're sensitive to heat), cumin, sugar, vinegar, a bit of salt, and broth to the pot, cover, reduce heat to medium-low, and simmer for 45 minutes.

After 45 minutes, remove from heat. Taste the broth, and adjust seasoning as necessary. Remove the chicken thighs and shred them by pulling in opposite directions with two forks.

When the chicken is all shredded, place it in a serving dish, spoon the sauce and onions over the top, and squeeze half a lime over the serving dish.

Serve with warm tortillas, sour cream, cilantro, and diced or pickled onions.

CHILAQUILES

Chilaquiles are, at their root, a dish to use up stale tortillas. Extra corn tortillas from the night before are fried and then simmered in a rich sauce. It may sound dull, but it will surprise you, particularly if you take the time to make your own sauce. The tortillas soak up all that delicious flavor and become the perfect accompaniment to fried eggs, shredded chicken, or just cheese and sour cream.

INGREDIENTS:

Simple Enchilada Sauce:
2 tbsp neutral oil
2 tbsp flour
3 tbsp chili powder (buy the good stuff)
½ tsp garlic powder
¼ tsp ground cumin
¼ tsp oregano
2 cups vegetable or chicken stock
1 tsp white vinegar
Salt, to taste

Chilaquiles:
6 corn tortillas
½ cup enchilada sauce
Neutral Oil
Salt, to taste

DIRECTIONS:

Simple Enchilada Sauce:
Make a blonde roux with the oil and flour over medium heat until it is just cooked. Add the spices and allow them to toast for 30-60 seconds. Add the stock and stir until there are no lumps. Allow the sauce to reduce for 15 minutes until you have around 12 ounces. Add salt and vinegar or lime juice to taste (around ½ tsp salt and 1 tsp vinegar/lime juice).

Chilaquiles:
The tortillas can be baked or fried. Cut them into triangles. For the oven, brush them with oil and bake at 350 until nice and crunchy. To fry, bring a small amount of oil to medium heat and fry until crisp. Salt liberally.

If you don't happen to have stale tortillas on hand, or are looking for a very quick breakfast, you can also use store-bought tortilla chips. Just opt for chips on the heartier side.

Heat the enchilada sauce in a pan over medium heat. Once hot, add the chips in and toss to get an even coating on all sides. They do not need to cook for long. Divide these between two plates and top with your choice of the many great chilaquiles toppings like shredded chicken, sour cream, avocado pieces, fried eggs, crumbled queso fresco, chopped fresh cilantro, lime juice, and hot sauce.

CAMARONES AL TEQUILA

Shrimp sautéed with tequila, fresh lime juice, and plenty of chili powder are perfect atop a bed of rice or wrapped in a warm tortilla. Just make sure you get plenty or shrimp, as they are quick to prepare and even quicker to eat.

Seafood is not always the easiest thing to cook when living the buslife. A lot of the areas we travel in are far from the ocean and lack good grocery stores, but shrimp are reliable. Even in the center of the driest desert, you can always buy a bag of frozen shrimp and whip up some quick, delicious shrimp tacos. Even in our little bus, we live in luxurious times. Bring on the desert seafood and tequila.

INGREDIENTS:

1 lb. shrimp, shelled
4 cloves garlic, minced
1 tbsp chili powder
½ tsp ground cumin
¼ cup tequila
¼ cup lime juice
2 tbsp butter
2 tbsp neutral oil

DIRECTIONS:

Cook the garlic over medium heat in 2 tbsp neutral oil until nicely fragrant. Add the spices and shrimp, and cook for 2 minutes. Add the tequila and cook for 1 minute. Add the lime juice and cook for 1 minute. Remove from heat, add the butter, and toss once melted. Salt to taste. Simple, simple.

Serve with warm tortillas, queso fresco, chopped cilantro, avocado, and lime wedges, or over Mexican rice with salad.

ARROZ CON LECHE

Arroz con Leche is Mexican rice pudding made by simmering rice with water and milk, allowing it to slowly take in moisture and release starches until the grains are tender and float in a beautiful pudding. Cloves, cinnamon, and a bit of sugar add sweetness and complexity, making this a simple and delicious dessert that (bonus) you probably have the ingredients to make right now. It has become one of our go-to recipes when we are craving sweets and don't have anything else on hand, and it also makes a great breakfast.

INGREDIENTS:

½ cup long grain rice
2 cups milk
¾ cup water
¼ tsp ground cinnamon
¼ tsp ground cloves
⅛ cup sugar
Pinch of salt
2 tbsp raisins (optional)

DIRECTIONS:

Put the rice in a skillet and add ¾ cup water. Bring the water to a boil with the rice, then reduce the heat to medium and cook until the water is mostly absorbed. Add the cinnamon and cloves.

Add ½ cup milk and simmer, stirring often, until it is mostly absorbed. Repeat this process until all the milk is used. If you are using raisins, add them just before the last ½ cup of milk. After the final addition of milk, reduce the heat to low and cook to the desired consistency.

When all the milk has been absorbed (at least as much as you want for a nice pudding consistency), remove from heat. Add the salt and sugar and stir to combine well. If you like things sweet, add more sugar to taste.

Garnish with a bit more cinnamon and a few raisins, and serve warm or cold.

WHAT IS "BUSLIFE?"

By now just about everyone with a smartphone has heard of vanlife. While it started long ago as a counterculture movement, living in vans has more recently been largely co-opted and sold to the world by social media influencers with brand-new, sparklingly clean Mercedes vans with price tags larger than a two-bedroom house. But that old, hippie spirit lives on in buslife. In place of expensive all-terrain cargo vans with six-figure builds, we have rusty old school buses in which we do our best to build a home. Bus conversions tend to be done by people like us, who go into it without much skill, experience, or money, all in pursuit of that same old dream. There are fewer showroom-worthy conversions, and it generally has a bit more grit about it, but the community is strong.

At its foundation, buslife and the more popular vanlife are just groups of people who love to travel and who choose to do so while living out of vans and buses, most of which have been converted into small, self-sufficient RVs. The practice is said to have started in the 1960s, with hippies living out of those famous VW buses, but it has grown quite a bit in scope and popularity in recent years. The stigma of the van down by the river is mostly gone, and it is becoming pretty mainstream. These days, the vanlife/buslife/rv community covers all sorts of varied demographics, but what unites us is a nomadic, minimalist lifestyle in which we have chosen to own less and thus have the freedom to experience more. Whether that means shredding powder all winter, chasing waves all summer, or just spending more time in the wild, a goal that we all share is creating more time and space to pursue the things that we are passionate about. For Ayana and me, that means hiking, trail running, paddle boarding, and lots of other outdoor sports, but also just spending our lives outside. Living in the bus, we get to explore a new backyard each week. We've camped in the sun-baked heart of the desert, high in the mountains surrounded by spruce

trees, and on beaches where we could practically step out our door and into the surf. We are free to travel to and live just about anywhere we want and stay for as long or as short as we like. On top of all that, living in the bus allows us to abscond from many of the expenses of modern life, which creates freedom for us to pursue the work that we are really passionate about. I am free to spend my days cooking, writing, reading, and taking photos, while Ayana crafts silver jewelry and practices natural dreamwork. For both of us, these pursuits are life-affirming, but they were hard to make time for or see as viable career options when the bills were coming as fast as they used to.

Despite the incredible freedom and adventure of buslife, I don't want you to walk away after reading this thinking that it's all rainbows and puppy dogs. There are plenty of difficulties baked into the lifestyle as well. Being on the move all the time, as romantic and charming as it is, can also be exhausting. Home is comfortable, and sometimes we definitely miss the stability of a house with hot showers, unlimited electricity, wifi capable of a full-day TV binge, or the space of a second room. Our bus is only around 90 square feet, which is smaller than many bedrooms, and

two of us and a puggle not only live our lives in there, but also have to find room to store all of our belongings. We eat, sleep, and work in that tiny space every day, and when it's rainy, windy, or cold out, there is no escape.

Living off-grid, monitoring our resource use is also a never-ending job. If the water tank runs dry at the end of the day, it's either time to run to town for a refill, or accept that we aren't drinking any water until tomorrow. If the house batteries get too low, the fridge stops running, and the food spoils. While it is very cool and enlightening to have such specific awareness of our resource use, being responsible for all of it adds a layer of difficulty to nearly every task. We are exceptionally careful with our use of water and electricity, in such a way that when we visit someone's house or get a hotel for the night, it feels almost gross to see how much goes to waste on a daily basis. Once you start hauling your own water, the concept of a flush toilet suddenly makes a whole lot less sense.

The largest difficulty of buslife, however, the one that is always looming behind us, breathing down our necks, is the inevitable breakdown. Especially with bus conversions, which tend to be older vehicles, there will be breakdowns. There are always things malfunctioning, and parts that need to be replaced. And, when the breakdowns come, it's not just your car going to the shop, it's also your house.

It is certainly a different way of living, this buslife, and it's not for everyone. There is enormous beauty in it, and so much freedom, but there are also plenty of difficulties. Many creature comforts must be left behind when you start living on the road. But, when you start to let go of the luxuries of modern life, something magical happens: you find the essentials. In the bus there is no longer any room for the things you sort of like, or that you might someday explore. All of the excess must be trimmed in order to fit into that tiny space, and you are left with only the things that matter most. That's the real beauty of it.

CHINESE RECIPES

SICHUAN CHILI OIL

After reading this recipe, you will have no choice but to start making your own chili oil. Store-bought chili oil is not only bland and boring, it's not even very spicy. At home, you can make a far superior batch of chili oil in five minutes that will last you months. You also have full control over the flavor profile, which means that you can make it complex, aromatic, and as spicy as you like. At the base, all you need is dried Chinese chilies, oil, and a bit of salt, but you can infuse huge amounts of flavor with the addition of things like: sichuan pepper, star anise, bay leaves, garlic, ginger, sesame seeds, scallions, cloves, cinnamon, 5-spice, et cetera.

INGREDIENTS:

½ cup dried chinese chilies, crushed and with most seeds removed (unless you like it really fiery)
1 tsp sichuan peppercorns
2 cloves garlic, smashed
1 cup neutral, high-heat oil (like vegetable or grapeseed)
Salt, to taste

DIRECTIONS:

Chop the dried chilies into small pieces. This process will release all the seeds, at least half of which should be discarded. If you are sensitive to heat, try to get rid of all the seeds (it'll still probably taste pretty spicy).

Put the chilies, peppercorns, and garlic in a heat-safe bowl, such as an ovenproof ceramic.

In a small pot heat your oil to around 370-380 degrees. Slowly pour the hot oil into the bowl over your other ingredients. It will sizzle and bubble gently and release a delightful aroma that smells a bit like popcorn. Stir things around and add a bit of salt while it is bubbling.

When it has cooled, cover and allow to steep for 24 hours at room temperature. The following day, remove anything that adds water to the mixture, such as garlic, ginger, or scallions, as these will go rancid. Without those ingredients, chili oil keeps a long time unrefrigerated.

EGG FLOWER SOUP

Egg drop soup, also called egg flower soup, is about as simple as it gets: a nice broth, lightly thickened with starch, and filled with lovely ribbons of egg. It's easy to make at home, and is something that we eat pretty regularly because it is delicious, warming, and we nearly always have the ingredients on hand (you probably do too). After you read this recipe, and see its simplicity, you will no longer have an excuse not to make egg drop soup every time you cook Chinese food.

INGREDIENTS:

6 cups chicken broth
2 tbsp cornstarch
¼ tsp white pepper
½ tsp sesame oil
¼ tsp garlic powder
¼ tsp ground ginger
1 tsp sugar
1 tsp chinkiang or rice vinegar
2 eggs, beaten
2 scallions, thinly sliced, to garnish

DIRECTIONS:

Make a slurry of 2 tbsp cornstarch and 2 tbsp water. Pour the slurry into the cold broth while stirring. Add the white pepper as well.

Bring the broth to a rolling boil over high heat, stirring often. Once boiling, reduce heat to medium.

Stir aggressively in a circle to create motion in the broth and slowly pour in the beaten eggs in a thin stream while continuing to stir. The speed of the whirlpool will decide the size of your egg ribbons—the faster you stir, the smaller they will be. Make them as large or as small as you like.

Remove from heat, add sesame oil, adjust seasonings as needed, and serve hot. Garnish with scallion greens.

Bang bang chicken is traditionally a street food or snack, made with poached and shredded chicken which is then tossed in "strange flavor" sauce. It is also often served as an appetizer over a bed of julienned cucumber. The strange flavor sauce is both spicy and numbing, from its use of fiery chili oil and the lip-tingling Sichuan peppercorns.

The name bang bang is derived from the traditional method of preparation, wherein the chicken would be poached and then split apart with a stick/baton/club, which is pronounced "Bàng" in Mandarin. This dish may also be called simply strange flavor chicken.

INGREDIENTS:

Chicken:
1.5 lbs. chicken thighs
4 scallions
2 tbsp neutral oil
Salt

Sauce:
4 tbsp soy sauce
2 tbsp Chinese sesame paste
2 tbsp chili oil
1.5 tbsp chinkiang vinegar
1 tbsp sugar
2 tsp garlic, minced
2 tsp ginger, grated
1 tsp Sichuan pepper, ground

DIRECTIONS:

Heat a large pan with a lid over high heat. Add 2 tablespoons of neutral oil, then the chicken thighs. Add salt and drape the scallions over the chicken. Cover the pan.

Cook on high heat until the bottom of the chicken is nicely browned, then flip, allowing the scallions to cook in the oil. Cook until the other side of the chicken is also nicely browned. Turn off the heat and allow the chicken to cool. It should be cooked through, but if you are nervous, you can slice a piece to check. Once cooled, shred the chicken.

Combine all sauce ingredients in a bowl and stir until sugar is dissolved and the sauce is a uniform consistency. Pour the sauce over the shredded chicken and mix well, evenly distributing the sauce.

Garnish with additional chili oil and thinly sliced scallion greens.
Serve by itself or with julienned cucumbers as an appetizer. Add rice for a full meal.

STEAMED DUMPLINGS

Is there any meal more delightful than a big plate of dumplings? If there is, I'm yet to meet it. Each two-bite morsel, dipped in a delicious sauce, is a little taste of perfection. A night of cooking and eating dumplings by the batch is a night well-spent, especially as a date night. The process works best with two people in the kitchen to manage the myriad tasks of rolling wrappers, making the filling, stuffing them, and steaming them, so it's a good one to cook together. Every eight minutes or so you get to take a break and enjoy a few magical bites. And you just keep going until you're full. It's a wonderful way to eat.

INGREDIENTS:

Filling:
1 lb. chicken thighs, minced
½ cup water chestnut, diced
½ scallions, sliced thinly
½ tsp white pepper
2 tbsp sweet soy sauce
2 tbsp soy sauce
1 tsp sesame oil

Wrappers:
2 cups flour
¾ hot water (best if just boiled)
Pinch of salt

Dipping Sauce:
2 tbsp water
2 tbsp soy sauce
2 tbsp chinkiang vinegar
1 tsp sesame oil
1 tsp chili oil
1 tsp sugar

DIRECTIONS:

Wrapper Dough:
Add the salt to the flour in a large mixing bowl. Slowly add water while stirring until well-mixed. Knead the dough briefly to ensure all flour is incorporated. If too dry, add water a few drops at a time. Once incorporated, knead for two minutes. Wrap in plastic and rest at room temperature for 30 minutes, or in the fridge overnight.

Filling:
Mince the chicken and scallions and dice the water chestnuts. Mix all the filling ingredients together in the appropriate measures in a large bowl.

Assembly:
Roll out your wrappers as thin as you are comfortable with and use a pint glass or rocks glass to cut circles. Spoon about one tablespoon of the filling into each wrapper. Wet one side of the wrapper, fold it up, and pinch it shut.

Cooking:
Steam the dumplings for 8 minutes, or until cooked through.

Dipping Sauce:
Mix together all ingredients and stir until the sugar dissolves.

Mapo Tofu is a stir-fried dish of ground meat and soft tofu in a vibrantly red spicy and numbing sauce made with sichuan peppercorns, roasted dried chilies, and doubanjiang. This dish, which hails from Sichuan province in China, is strong, fiery, and exceptionally delicious.

The name mapo translates literally to "pock-marked grandma," with ma meaning "pock," and po meaning "elderly woman" or "grandma." The story goes that it was invented by and named after an unfortunately disfigured woman with the surname Chen who ran a restaurant in Chengdu in the 1860s. While the history is not completely certain, there are records of that restaurant, Chen Mapo Tofu Restaurant, dating from the early 1900s, and there is still a restaurant by that name in Chengdu to this day.

INGREDIENTS:

½ lb. ground pork
1 lb. silken or soft tofu, cut to 1" cubes
¼ cup neutral oil
8 dried chinese chilies (fewer if you are sensitive to spice)
2 tbsp sichuan peppercorns
3 tbsp garlic, minced
3 tbsp ginger, grated or minced
2 tbsp chili bean paste (doubanjiang)
1 cup chicken broth
1½ tsp cornstarch mixed with ¼ cup water
1 tsp sugar
2 scallions, sliced thinly

DIRECTIONS:

Add the oil to a wok or large skillet over medium heat. When hot, add the chilies and sichuan peppercorns and fry until fragrant and the chilies begin to darken.

Add the ginger and garlic and fry until nicely fragrant, being careful not to burn it.

Add the pork, break it up, stir all together, and cook until the pork is just done.

Add the chili bean sauce and sugar, and stir together to mix well. Add the broth and then the cornstarch slurry. Stir together until slightly thickened.

Remove the pan from heat. Add the scallions and tofu, and stir together gently, being careful not to pulverize the soft tofu cubes.

Serve with rice.

STEWED PORK BELLY OVER RICE

This recipe was reverse-engineered from a dish at one of my favorite restaurants in Boulder. I believe it is based off the Taiwanese dish lu rou fan. The pork belly is stewed in broth and becomes wonderfully unctuous and fragrant with the many spices. The broth is enriched by the fat from the pork belly, and together over rice they are truly spectacular: rich, aromatic, and delicious. With some quickly blanched baby bok choy and a boiled egg simmered in the broth, this is a truly magnificent meal.

INGREDIENTS:

1 lb. Pork belly, cut into 12 even pieces
2 cups light broth (chicken, vegetable, pork)
½ tsp chinese 5 spice powder
½ cup scallions, roughly chopped
4 eggs, boiled and peeled
3 tbsp soy sauce
1 tbsp rice vinegar
1" ginger, skinned and roughly chopped
2 cloves garlic, roughly chopped
1 tsp sugar
1 tsp black peppercorns
1 medium yellow onion
1 tbsp sweet soy sauce

DIRECTIONS:

Brown the pork in a large, heavy-bottomed pot over medium-high heat. When the pork belly is brown on all sides, add the onion, ginger, garlic, peppercorns, and half of the scallions, and cook for another 5 minutes until they are softened.

Add the broth and stir to scrape up any stuck bits of pork. Add all remaining ingredients (except that last ¼ cup of green onions) to the pot—this includes those boiled eggs. Reduce heat to low, cover, and allow to simmer for at least 2 hours.

Check in on it occasionally to ensure there is enough liquid left. Add boiling water if necessary. The sauce should reduce to a thick and rich broth—don't add too much water and end up with soup at the end. But also don't let the water run out and burn your sauce.

Serve over rice garnished with the remaining scallions.

SMASHED CUCUMBER SALAD

A light, crunchy salad of sliced and smashed cucumbers in a deliciously aromatic and well-balanced dressing. Like many Chinese dishes, this salad is the perfect balance of salty, sour, sweet, and spicy, and it makes an excellent side to just about anything.

INGREDIENTS:

2 english cucumbers
½ tsp salt
½ tsp sugar

Dressing:
1 ½ tbsp chinkiang vinegar
1 tsp chili oil
2 tsp soy sauce
½ tsp sugar
2 tsp sesame oil
½ tsp minced garlic
1 tbsp neutral oil
Salt to taste

Garnish:
2 cloves garlic, smashed, fried, and crumbled
Crushed red pepper or dried Chinese chilies to taste

DIRECTIONS:

Prep the cucumbers by quartering them, laying them seed side down on the cutting board, and smashing them with the side of your knife. This breaks down the cucumber slightly to create a better texture and allow the dressing to marinate more fully.

Then slice the cucumbers into ½" pieces and put them in a strainer. Add ½ tsp salt and ½ tsp sugar, mix well, and leave to drain over a bowl for 30 minutes.

To make the dressing, simply combine the ingredients and mix well to ensure the sugar dissolves.

When your cucumbers have drained, put them in a container, pour the dressing over, and put the container in the refrigerator for at least 30 minutes (but you can do this hours ahead or even the day before). Taste and add additional salt now, if desired.

Serve garnished with crumbled crispy fried garlic and crushed red pepper, if desired.

KUNG PAO CHICKEN

Kung Pao chicken, alternatively known as Gong Bao Chicken, is a stir-fried dish made with cubed chicken, peanuts, and a sweet and sour "lychee flavor" sauce. This particular recipes falls somewhere between authentic and Americanized: the flavors are authentic, but I've padded out meal with onion and green bell pepper pieces. It's quick, delicious, and better than the cheap Chinese takeout down the road.

INGREDIENTS:

1 lb. chicken breast, cubed
5 scallion whites, sliced thin
1 green pepper, diced large
½ white onion, diced large
12 dried Chinese chilies
1 tsp Sichuan peppercorns
2 tbsp garlic, minced
2 tbsp ginger, grated
½ cup roasted peanuts
4 tbsp neutral oil

Marinade:
2 tsp Chinkiang vinegar
2 tbsp soy sauce
2 tsp rice wine

Sauce:
1 tbsp soy sauce
1 tbsp sweet soy sauce
2 tbsp chinkiang vinegar
1½ tbsp water
1 tbsp sugar
1½ tsp cornstarch
1 tsp sesame oil

DIRECTIONS:

Cube the chicken breast and allow it to marinate for at least 15 minutes before cooking. During this time, make the sauce in a small bowl by combining the soy sauce, sweet soy sauce, chinkiang vinegar, water, sugar, cornstarch, and sesame oil. Mix this together well and set it aside for later.

In a large skillet, heat 4 tablespoons of neutral oil over medium heat. When hot, add the dried chilies and sichuan peppercorns. Toast these until they are nicely fragrant and the chilies begin to darken. Add the cubed chicken breast, onion, and green pepper. Stir this all together and cook until the chicken breast is just done (you can slice a piece if you are unsure).

Next add the ginger, garlic, scallions, and peanuts. Stir this together and cook until wonderfully fragrant.

Add the sauce to the pan and stir until it thickens. Remove from heat.

Serve over rice, garnished with thinly sliced scallion greens.

VEGAN RECIPES

BALSAMIC GLAZED BEETS

I chose this recipe to start the vegan section of my cookbook because it makes an important point about vegan food: vegan recipes don't need to be complicated or rely on substitutes. I put this recipe together for a dinner party I was hosting made entirely from vegetables I grew in my garden. It had been a good year for beets, and I had them coming out of my ears. Many people are put off by the earthy flavor of beets, so I wanted something that could play well there, and landed on a lemony balsamic glaze. It is still, to my knowledge, the only time that my cooking has brought someone to tears. Hearing that a dish is vegan food or contains beets turns a lot of people off, but I think that this recipe might just open their minds.

INGREDIENTS:

2 lbs. beets (I prefer mild chioggias, but any variety will do)
½ cup balsamic vinegar
2 tsp sugar
1 tsp lemon zest
olive oil
salt, to taste

DIRECTIONS:

Peel the beets, dice large, and toss with olive oil and salt. Roast at 450 degrees for around 90 minutes, until browning around the edges. Remove from the oven to cool a bit. Alternatively, if you don't have an oven, blanch the cubed beets until tender, then drain, dry, and saute until the edges are browned.

The beets can be cooked in advance if necessary, just be sure to reheat them before glazing.

To make the glaze, add the balsamic vinegar and sugar to a saucepan and reduce until syrupy. Once you reach the desired consistency, drop the beets into the pan and toss to cover with glaze.

Remove the beets to a serving dish and sprinkle with lemon zest and salt and pepper to taste.

TOFU ADOBO

Adobo is considered by many to be the unofficial national dish of the Philippines. There are said to be as many ways to make adobo as there are Filipino households, though precious few of them are vegan. Like many coastal Asian cuisines, a large percentage of Filipino dishes include some quantity of meat, fish, or both. I came up with this recipe for a birthday dinner for Ayana's mother. She spent two years in the Philippines with the Peace Corps, and loves adobo, but for this birthday dinner she did not want to eat any meat. While it may not be the most traditional option out there, this mushroom and tofu adobo is a delicious vegan alternative, which might just have you skipping the meat next time too.

INGREDIENTS:

1 box firm tofu (~14 oz.)
12 oz. crimini mushrooms, thickly sliced
cornstarch
3 cloves garlic, minced
1 small yellow onion, quartered and sliced
1 large serrano pepper, sliced thin
1 tbsp sweet soy sauce or brown sugar
¾ cup soy sauce
½ cup white vinegar
1 tbsp black pepper
2 bay leaves

DIRECTIONS:

Make a marinade with the soy, sweet soy, vinegar, garlic, serrano, black pepper, and bay leaves. Marinate the mushrooms for 30 minutes.

Drain the tofu and slice it into bite-sized pieces. Dry it with a paper towel and coat it with cornstarch, then pan fry in a neutral oil over medium-high heat. Once golden brown and crispy on the outside, set aside to drain.

Cook the onion in a large pot over medium-high heat with a splash of oil until fragrant, then add the marinade and mushrooms to the pot. Allow the marinade to reduce slightly (~5 min), then add the tofu. Reduce the sauce for 5 more minutes. Remove from heat.

Serve with rice.

WATERMELON GAZPACHO

In the heat of summer, there is no better way to start a meal than with a nice watermelon gazpacho, a small serving of cool soup with that incredible combination of summer flavors: watermelon and mint. This gazpacho is refreshing and screams healthy at you while you sip it—preferably alongside a mojito or mint julep to counterbalance all those nutrients.

INGREDIENTS:

3 cups watermelon, cubed
1 cucumber, peeled, seeded, and coarsely chopped
3 roma tomatoes, seeded and coarsely chopped
½ red onion, coarsely chopped
2 cloves garlic
¼ cup mint, lightly packed
3 tbsp olive oil
3 tbsp white wine vinegar
1 tsp salt
½ tsp black pepper
¼ tsp cumin
1 cup stale bread, soaked and drained (optional)

DIRECTIONS:

Soak your stale bread in water for a few minutes to rehydrate it.

Peel, seed, and coarsely chop all your vegetables and toss them in a blender with the spices and oil. When this is done, take the rehydrated bread, squeeze out most of the water, and toss it in the blender as well. You can make the gazpacho without the bread, but it will not have the same silkiness. Blend the ingredients until smooth.

Next you will strain the gazpacho. Pour the soup in batches through a fine sieve. This part is technically optional, but if you do not strain the gazpacho it has what I consider to be an unpleasant, grainy mouthfeel. With each batch, get as much liquid through as you can and then rinse the solids from the sieve.

Once the gazpacho is strained, place it in the fridge for an hour or two to allow the flavors to meld and the soup to chill.

Best served in small portions (~6 oz.) with a few crunchy bits on the top, such as croutons.

Falafel is made from ground chickpeas, spices, and herbs which are formed into balls or patties and fried or baked. The resulting cakes are crisp, aromatic, savory, and filling. They are equally good served as part of a mezze platter with hummus and baba ganoush, or stuffed into a pita with lettuce and dressing. When making falafel at home, the trick is in the moisture of the chickpeas. Soaking dried chickpeas overnight gets them just where you want them, not too moist and not too dry.

INGREDIENTS:

1 cup dried chickpeas, soaked overnight
½ yellow onion
1 cup fresh parsley
1 cup fresh cilantro
1 tsp cumin
1 tsp salt
¼ tsp fresh black pepper
2 tbsp flour (or chickpea flour for GF)
Neutral oil to pan fry

DIRECTIONS:

Soak the chickpeas overnight to reach the perfect moisture content.

Drain the chickpeas and add them to the food processor along with the onion and herbs. Grind them up until the texture is reminiscent of wet sand. When the mixture reaches the right consistency, add the spices, salt, and flour, and mix together. Rest for 15 minutes to allow the flour to rehydrate.

Falafel can be baked or deep fried, but I prefer a simple pan fry. Add a few tablespoons of oil to a heavy-bottomed skillet and heat over medium to medium-high heat. Form patties about ¾ of an inch thick and 2-3 inches in diameter. Place them carefully into the oil and fry for ~2 minutes on each side, until a nice brown crust forms. The mixture is very fragile until that crust forms, but once they've been cooked on both sides, they are quite durable.

These are great in a pita sandwich, on a platter with hummus, or just eaten by themselves as a snack.

CHIPOTLE BLACK BEAN HUMMUS

The base of hummus is no more than cooked beans mixed with oils, flavorings, and a paste of seeds or nuts. I have tried many different flavors, using chickpeas, cannellini beans, black beans, tahini, peanut butter, all sorts of things, and this chipotle black bean hummus is one of the best. Black beans make a very creamy hummus, and the chipotles add a delicious southwestern flavor for when you need a break from that same old hummus recipe. But replace the black beans with chickpeas, take out the chipotles, and swap the limes for lemon, and there's the classic recipe for you.

INGREDIENTS:

1 can black beans
½ cup tahini
¼ cup olive oil
¼ tsp cumin
2 cloves of garlic
2-3 chipotles in adobo, depending on your spice tolerance
¼ cup cilantro
Juice of 2-3 limes

DIRECTIONS:

Toss all of the ingredients into a food processor and puree until smooth. This hummus should come out very creamy, but if it is too thick, add water 1 tbsp at a time until the desired consistency is reached.

Serve with sliced vegetables, pita, or tortilla chips.

VEGAN POKE BOWL

While poke is traditionally made from raw fish, the word actually just means to slice crosswise, so I think this vegan option still qualifies. Substituting cubes of tender, boiled beets creates a dish with a similar look to ahi tuna, and a surprisingly similar flavor profile. Whether you eat a vegan diet or you simply don't have access to sushi-grade fish where you are, give this recipe a try next time that poke bowl craving hits you.

INGREDIENTS:

Poke:
~3 cups of beets, cut into ½" cubes (around 2 large beets)
¼ cup soy sauce
2 tbsp rice vinegar
2 tsp sesame oil
2 tsp sugar
1 tsp grated ginger
2 scallions, white parts only, sliced thin

Sushi Rice:
See page 136

Accoutrements:
1 cup cucumber, seeded and diced
1 cup avocado, diced
1 carrot, peeled and sliced into thin sticks
2 scallion greens sliced thin
2 tbsp toasted sesame seeds
½ cup sriracha mayonnaise (50:50 sriracha:mayo)

DIRECTIONS:

Poke: In a large bowl, combine the soy sauce, sesame oil, sugar, rice vinegar, ginger, and scallion whites to make the marinade.

Peel beets and slice into ½"-1" cubes. Boil the beet cubes for 20-30 minutes, or until tender. Once cooked, drain the beets and drop them into the marinade. Marinate for at least 30 minutes, stirring occasionally.

Sushi rice:
See recipe on page 136

Poke Bowl Assembly:
Divide the rice evenly into 4 bowls, creating a nice layer at the bottom. Mix the sliced carrots, cubed cucumber, and avocado into the beet poke, and divide this evenly atop the bed of sushi rice. Give the bowls a nice squirt of sriracha mayonnaise and sprinkle over the toasted sesame seeds and scallion greens. And then dig in.

For a more photogenic bowl, reserve the cucumber, carrot, and avocado and arrange them artfully on top of the rice. The beets and marinade will stain the other vegetables red.

THAI YELLOW CURRY TOFU

When it comes to vegan Thai curries, unless you are making your own paste at home, you really only have the one option: yellow. While curry is a perfect dish for vegetables and tofu, red, green, panang, and massaman curry pastes all typically include some quantity of shrimp paste. So, what makes yellow curry different?

The name for this Thai dish, Kaeng Kari, which translates to "curry curry," is a good indicator of its origins and why it differs from other Thai curries. The origins of this dish lie with "curry powder," a British attempt to bottle the curries of India. Kaeng Kari is made by adding curry powder (or its various spices) to a traditional Thai curry base of chile, garlic, shallot, galangal, lemongrass, and cilantro root. The resulting curry may not be the traditional southern Thai yellow curry, but it is both vegan and definitely delicious enough to cement its place in Thai cuisine, as it has done both in Thailand and abroad.

INGREDIENTS:

1 yellow onion, quartered and sliced thin
1 package extra firm tofu, sliced
1 red bell pepper, sliced thin
1 green bell pepper, sliced thin
4 small yukon gold potatoes, cubed and parboiled
2 carrots, sliced medium thin
3 crimini mushrooms, sliced
1 can bamboo shoots, drained
4 tbsp yellow curry paste
2 cans coconut milk
1 kaffir lime leaf

Finish with:
1 tbsp peanut butter
1 tbsp soy sauce
1.5 tsp sugar
2 tsp lime juice

DIRECTIONS:

Saute vegetables over medium heat in a small amount of neutral oil until slightly softened but not colored. Add curry paste and cook for around 1 minute. Add coconut milk, potatoes, and kaffir lime leaf, cover, and simmer until vegetables are tender. Add tofu and simmer for 5 minutes more.

Remove from heat, and stir in peanut butter, soy sauce, sugar, and lime juice.

Serve over rice.

Pudding is one of my favorite desserts to scratch-make in the bus. Not only is it simple to make, it is just as simple to make vegan. A basic stovetop pudding is really just about adding sugar and flavoring to a milk (dairy or non-dairy, doesn't matter), adding cornstarch, and then simmering it to the correct temperature.

INGREDIENTS:

3 cups soy milk (or other preferred milk)
1 cup dark chocolate (check packaging to ensure it does not contain dairy)
¼ cup sugar
¼ cup cornstarch
Pinch of salt

DIRECTIONS:

In a small bowl, combine ¼ cup cornstarch and ¼ cup soy milk, and make a paste. When a smooth paste is achieved, add another ¼ cup soy milk and stir to mix well.

In a saucepan, combine the remaining soy milk with the dark chocolate, sugar, and a pinch of salt over medium-low heat. Stir the mixture until the chocolate is melted. Check the temperature with a thermometer. Anything below 160 degrees is acceptable. Give your cornstarch slurry a quick stir and pour it into the saucepan. Stir to combine.

Continue stirring the pot and keeping an eye on the temperature as it increases. Be especially sure to regularly scrape the bottom, as this heats first, and can create lumps in your pudding. At around 160 degrees, the pudding will begin to thicken. When you reach 170, the pudding is fully thickened and should be immediately removed from heat. If you do not have a thermometer, you can judge the doneness of your pudding by its consistency. When it coats the back of a spoon, it is done.

Refrigerate the pudding for several hours to allow it to properly set. A piece of plastic wrap set directly on the surface of the pudding will prevent it forming a skin in the refrigerator.

STOVETOP BAKING

When we were planning our build, for whatever reason, we could not find any good information about ovens for the bus. We found a few vanlife articles, but in every case the person was jury-rigging an oven that was explicitly intended only for outdoor use into their indoor kitchen. The installations involved lots of work and tons of space, and frankly seemed dangerous. For the sake of safety and simplicity we opted for a 3-burner propane cooktop, and I vowed that I would learn to bake on the stove.

Of course, as soon as we finished our build we started finding articles all over the place about RV ovens. But, realistically, even if we had known about them, we likely wouldn't have put one in. The space taken up by an oven, particularly one that is safely heat-shielded, would have meant making big sacrifices elsewhere. While it might not have changed our design, finding all those ovens that we'd somehow missed before did really light a fire under me to learn how to bake on the stove.

If you follow the vanlife or buslife community, you might be familiar with the Omnia stove-top oven. It looks a bit like a bundt pan with a silicone liner. I initially considered buying one of these, but, stubborn tinkerer that I am, I couldn't think of a reason that I wouldn't be able to engineer something better using only the tools already in our kitchen, and not need to spend $100 on yet another specialized tool which we would also need to make space for in the cabinet. You'd be amazed how much of our storage is already consumed by cooking equipment–we definitely don't need to add anything else.

Over the next few pages you will find my solution broken down into equipment and technique. While this is definitely not the only way to bake on a stove, we have been really happy with both

the simplicity and the results. We make pizza probably once a week, but we also love to bake cookies, pies, biscuits—I even roasted a Thanksgiving turkey! Hopefully this guide saves you some trouble and helps you bake up some tasty treats.

EQUIPMENT LIST:

Cast iron pan with lid
Wire cooling rack
10-inch baking trays
9-inch cake pans
Stove thermometer

BASICS:

The process is actually pretty simple. All you do is heat the cast-iron pan with the lid on and the wire rack inside until it reaches the desired temperature, and then toss in the food on a baking sheet, just like you would in a normal oven. You can stick the stove thermometer to the side of the pan to know when you've hit your desired temp. The only real differences between this and a conventional oven are that temperature control isn't automatic and you need to create both an air gap around your food and a means to vent steam. I'll go over each of these in a bit more detail below.

TEMPERATURE MANAGEMENT:

When I started baking on the stove, I did it entirely by touch. When I could only touch the lid for a second or two, I knew that things were pretty hot inside. It wasn't until a few months in that I remembered that we had a magnetic thermometer stuck to the side of our wood stove which was perfect for this task (and perhaps even more accurate than my finger technique).

Once that issue was solved, everything started to be a lot more precise. Not that I had any problems before. I made pizzas, pies, and a Thanksgiving turkey using only the touch technique, but as someone who is constantly working on recipes, the tighter I can get my data, the better. So, I would strongly advise spending the $10 or so to get a thermometer for the side of your pot.

AIR GAP:

The big difference between oven baking and other methods of cooking is the form of heat applied. Remember those from physics class back in the day? There are three types of heat: radiant, conductive, and convective. Radiant heat is transferred through electromagnetic waves, convective heat is transferred via liquids and gases, and conductive heat is transferred through solids. When cooking in a skillet, the heat is largely conductive, as it is transferred directly from the hot pan into your food. In an oven, the food is cooked by all three forms of heat: the outside of the oven gets hot and transfers radiant heat; the pan on which the food sits heats and transfers conductive heat; but, most importantly, the hot air in the oven cooks the food via convective heat.

Ovens apply dry heat to food and do so more gradually and evenly. If you put a whole chicken in a skillet for an hour, it will be burned on one side and raw on the other. An oven, on the other hand, cooks from all sides, creating a beautiful roasted bird. The air gap in the oven is what allows that dry heat to work. A little wire cooling rack does the trick just fine with our stovetop setup, reducing the conductive heat transfer and allowing things to bake without burning on the bottom.

STEAM VENTING:

The pan that we use to bake on the stovetop has a little pouring spout on either side, which makes a perfect steam vent for baking, but sticking a wooden skewer under the lid on one side of a pot works just as well. The degree to which you need to vent steam varies based on what you are cooking. If you are baking something with a lot of liquid in it and you don't have a sufficient vent, it will start dripping back onto itself, which can really mess up the texture of things like pies.

That's really all there is to it. Heat your pan with the wire rack inside and lid on until it reaches your desired temperature, then pop in your food on a baking sheet and bake for however long it says in the recipe. And, like a traditional oven, try not to check on it too often, as you will lose a lot of heat every time you open it up. For more information, check out the product list (and lots of other resources) at thebuslifekitchen.com

BAKING RECIPES

Pizza was the first buslife baking task I set out to perfect. It's easy enough, and even when it isn't perfect, it's still pizza. This picture up top is the very first one I did in the bus. See? Easy as pie.

INGREDIENTS:

Dough:
1 packet yeast
1 tsp sugar
3½ cups flour
1½ cups water
1 tsp salt
3 tbsp olive oil

Pizza:
8 oz. tomato sauce
8-12 oz. grated mozzarella
Oregano, to taste
Whatever other toppings you enjoy. Ayana likes pineapple and jalapeno person, but I prefer pepperoni and black olive.

DIRECTIONS:

Awaken the yeast by dissolving 1 tsp sugar into 1½ cups of warm water. Add the dried yeast and stir until it dissolves, and allow this mixture to sit a few minutes until the yeast begins to form a foam on the water's surface. Then add the 3 tbsp olive oil to the mixture.

Pour 3½ cups flour into a mixing bowl and stir in 2 tsp salt. Next add the bowl of water and yeast, and stir together until all the flour is taken up into the dough ball. Transfer the dough ball to a well-floured work surface and knead for around 4 minutes. Coat the dough lightly with oil, return it to the mixing bowl, and allow it to rise for at least an hour. But really, the longer the better. I usually start the dough around midday when we're having pizza for dinner.

Once risen, divide into fourths. Spread the dough out nice and thin on your baking tray and fold a little bit back on itself around the outside to make the crust.Add sauce, cheese, and toppings to the center. It is easy to overdo it when topping pizzas, so keep that in mind.

Bake at 450-500 for 10-15 minutes, or until crust is crisp and cheese is nicely melted. Makes four 9" personal pizzas.

This is the first pie recipe that I concocted in the bus, for our first Thanksgiving on the road. It took a few tries to get it just right, but using a graham cracker crust turned out to be exactly what we needed to make the perfect buslife pumpkin pie.

INGREDIENTS:

Ingredients:

Graham Cracker Crust:
11-12 graham crackers (around 1½ cups of crumbs)
2 tbsp brown sugar
4 tbsp butter

Pie filling:
1 can pumpkin puree
2 eggs
½ cup sugar
¾ tsp salt
1½ tsp pumpkin pie spice
1 cup evaporated milk

DIRECTIONS:

Graham Cracker Crust:
Add the graham crackers to a food processor and pulse until they are smashed into fine crumbs (or smash the graham crackers by hand in a large ziploc bag). In a small pan, melt the butter and dissolve the sugar into it. Add this mixture to your graham cracker crumbs and combine well. It should have a texture like wet sand.

Spread the mixture evenly around a 9" pie pan, and pack down the bottom and sides.

Pie Filling:
Beat the eggs well and add them to a mixing bowl along with all of the other ingredients (pumpkin puree, sugar, salt, evaporated milk, and spices). Mix this together until it is smooth and pour it into the pie pan over your crust.

Pie:
Bake the pie at 400 degrees. The pie is cooked when the temperature at the center reaches 175 degrees, but it will not be ruined if you go a little bit over. Try to remove it around 175-180, which should take 40-45 minutes.

Focaccia is an easy bread. It is always delicious and, unlike many breads, it doesn't require much finesse. While focaccia is closely associated with olive oil, there is no oil in the dough itself. Oil in dough makes it denser, so a lack of oil creates a soft, spongy texture. With the oiled pan and the oil drizzled over the top, it develops a delicious, crispy crust on all sides with an open crumb, all augmented by whatever decorations and additions you choose.

INGREDIENTS:

3 cups flour
1½ tsp salt
1 envelope yeast
1 tsp sugar
1½ cups water
¼ cup olive oil
2 cloves garlic
4 tsp herbs of your choice (basil, oregano, rosemary, etc.)
Other garnishes (kalamata olives, grape tomatoes, etc.)

DIRECTIONS:

Dissolve the sugar in a bowl of 1½ cups warm water. Add the dried yeast and stir, allowing it to dissolve. Set this aside for a few minutes until it is nice and foamy on top, indicating the yeast have activated.

In a large mixing bowl combine flour, salt, and 2 teaspoons of your dried herbs of choice. Mix well. Add the water and yeast, and stir until a dough ball forms. Knead it a couple of times to make a nice, uniform ball. Coat the ball with olive oil and place it back in the mixing bowl. Cover the bowl with a damp cloth or plastic wrap, and leave in a warm place to rise.

After a few hours, when the dough has doubled in size, punch it down and toss it onto a floured workspace. Form the dough into a nice ball, and then slice it in half. Knead the halves a couple times and form them into their own dough balls.

Heavily drizzle the bottom of two 9" cake pans with olive oil and add the dough balls, spreading the dough out evenly. Dimple the top deeply by poking your fingers into the dough. Poke hard, all the way to the bottom, but not through the dough. It should spring back, but leave a nice indentation.

Mince the garlic and scatter it over the top with your remaining 2 teaspoons of herbs. Pour over the remaining olive oil, and stud the bread with olives or tomatoes if you are using them. A sprinkling of coarse salt over the top is good too.

Bake at 450 for around 20-25 minutes until they are golden and crisp.

DROP BISCUITS

We all know that drop biscuits are the perfect accompaniment to a skillet of country gravy, but their use in the kitchen doesn't stop there. They're great with just about any breakfast, topped with butter and jam, but they're just as good alongside soups and stews. Add a little sugar and they're pretty good topped with strawberries and cream as well. For as little effort as these biscuits ask, they sure do deliver a lot of options.

INGREDIENTS:

4 cups flour
2 tbsp baking powder
1 stick butter
2 tsp salt
1 ½ cups milk
Optional:
2 tsp dried herbs
2 tsp black pepper
1 tsp garlic powder

DIRECTIONS:

Stir together the dry ingredients in a large mixing bowl.

Melt the butter, combine it with the milk, and add it to the dry ingredients. Stir into a uniform batter.

Spoon the batter onto a lightly greased baking sheet and bake at 400 degrees for around 15-20 minutes, or until baked through.

FRENCH RECIPES

FRENCH ONION SOUP

Ahh, French onion soup, that glorious bowl of caramelized onions in a rich, wine and herb-laced broth. It is a time-consuming dish to prepare, but worth every minute spent stirring those onions as they slowly brown and sweeten. Optionally topped with a slice of bread and melted comté, there are few better starters out there.

In the bus we do not have a broiler, which makes the addition of bread and melted cheese a bit more difficult, but I really don't miss them. The beauty of French onion soup is in the onions, not the cheese. Trust me when I tell you that eating this soup with just a bit of crusty bread on the side is every bit as good, you won't miss the comté for a second. But, if you've got to have that cheese, you can always use a butane torch to achieve the same effect.

INGREDIENTS:

4 lbs. yellow onions
1 cup sherry or dry white wine
4 tbsp butter
2 tbsp white wine vinegar
8 cups beef broth
2 tsp thyme
1 tsp pepper
Salt, to taste

DIRECTIONS:

Melt 4 tbsp butter in a large pot and caramelize the onions over medium heat. This is the most important part of the recipe, but it does mean standing by the stove and occasionally stirring the onions for up to an hour. Eventually, they will cook out enough water and start to turn a beautiful brown, enhancing their sweetness and fragrance.

When the onions are nice and caramelized, add the sherry and herbs to the pot and cook for a few minutes to allow the majority of the moisture to cook off.

Add the stock and allow it to reach a steady simmer, then simmer for at least 10 minutes. This can be put on the back burner for a long time, if you have other dishes to prepare.

Remove from heat and finish with 2 tbsp white wine vinegar and additional salt, to taste.

Garnish with freshly cracked black pepper, and the traditional crouton with comté, if desired.

STEAK AU POIVRE

Steak au Poivre is a classic French dish of pepper-crusted steak with a cognac and cream pan sauce. A crust of coarse, freshly ground pepper provides a zingy counterpoint to the beef, with the cream sauce adding sweetness and depth. It is undoubtedly delicious, and actually pretty easy to put together for such a show-stopping main course.

INGREDIENTS:

2 ribeyes, thick cut and around 1 lb. each
4 tbsp black peppercorns
1 large shallot, finely diced
2 tbsp butter
1 tsp dijon mustard
½ cup cognac or brandy
¾ cup cream
Salt, to taste

DIRECTIONS:

Pound the peppercorns under the side of a knife blade or in a mortar to a very coarse grind. Salt the ribeye liberally and then coat both sides in a thick crust of pepper.

Heat 1 tsp high-temperature oil in a cast iron skillet over medium-high heat. When nice and hot, add the steaks. Cook to your desired doneness, flipping halfway through. Once cooked, remove the steak to a cutting board and allow it to rest.

Reduce the heat to medium-low, and add the butter to the pan. Once melted, add your minced shallots and cook until slightly translucent and very fragrant. Add the cognac, and cook for a few minutes to reduce by around half.

Add the mustard, cream, and any steak juices from your resting dish. Reduce the sauce to you desired thickness, stirring often. Taste and add additional salt, if desired.

Slice the steaks, serving around half a steak on each plate with a nice strip of sauce down the center, and another sprinkle of salt to finish the meat.

GRATIN DAUPHINOIS

Gratin Dauphinois is an absolutely delicious, absolutely decadent potato dish that will knock everyone's socks off at your next vanlife gathering. Thinly sliced potatoes baked in rosemary-infused cream and topped with melted cheese, it is good enough to be a main course, but is even better alongside a roast chicken and some steamed vegetables.

INGREDIENTS:

3 lbs. Russet potatoes, peeled and sliced into ⅛" rounds
3 cloves garlic, minced
1½ cups cream
1½ cups whole milk
1 cup sour cream
1 tsp salt
1 tsp pepper
2 sprigs rosemary
1 cup grated swiss or gruyere cheese

DIRECTIONS:

Peel the potatoes and slice them into ⅛" rounds. This is the kind of task that will make you so happy to have that mandolin tucked away.

Add the cream, milk, sour cream, garlic, rosemary, salt, and pepper to a large saucepan or skillet over medium heat. When this begins to bubble, add the potatoes, return to a simmer, and cook for around 10 minutes.

After 10 minutes, remove the pan from heat, and layer your potatoes in a large baking dish. Remove and discard the rosemary sprigs, then pour the remaining cream over the potatoes. Top the potatoes with 1 cup of grated swiss or gruyere.

Bake at 400 for around 35-40 minutes, until the potatoes are fork-tender and the cheese on top is nicely melted.

Allow to cool for at least 5-10 minutes before serving.

This dish is a stovetop roast bird with herbs and lemon. After the bird is cooked, the vegetables and drippings are thickened with flour and pureed into a delicious lemon pan gravy. It was the main course at our first buslife Christmas dinner, the guests of which described the dish as delicious, clean, lemony, and bouncy. And who doesn't want a plate of bouncy chicken?

INGREDIENTS:

1 whole chicken (~5 lbs.)
3 tbsp olive oil
2 sprigs fresh rosemary
1 cup white wine
3 cups chicken broth
½ lemon
1 medium yellow onion, cut into sixths and sliced at ½" intervals
4 cloves garlic, peeled and crushed
3 ribs celery, sliced into ½" pieces
1 large carrot, sliced into ½" rounds
2 tbsp flour
Salt + Pepper, to taste

DIRECTIONS:

Spatchcock the bird by slicing down either side of the spine and removing it. Then lay the bird back down and spread it out. Apply pressure to the breast to open the cavity and allow the bird to lie flatter. Rub the skin side with oil, and salt both sides liberally. While doing this, start your roasting vessel, a large, heavy-bottomed pot over medium heat. When the pot is hot, sear the bird skin-side down until it has a nice color to it. Then remove the bird to a cutting board.

Add a bit of oil and the onion, garlic, celery, carrot, and rosemary to the pot. Cook, stirring regularly, until nicely fragrant and the onions begin to turn translucent. Then add the halved lemon as well as 1 cup of white wine and 1 cup of broth, set in your roasting rack, and place the bird on the rack skin side up. Cover the pot and roast for around 9 minutes per pound, until the internal temperature at the thickest part of the breast reads 165 degrees.

When the bird is cooked through, remove it from the pot to rest. Remove the roasting rack, rosemary sprigs, and lemon halves as well.

In a small bowl, make a slurry of 2 tbsp flour and 2 tbsp broth. When this slurry is well-mixed add it to the pot along with the remaining 2 cups of chicken broth. Stir this together and allow it to reach a boil and thicken for a few minutes, then remove from heat. Puree this with an immersion blender and adjust the seasoning as needed.

BOUEF BOURGUIGNON

On a cold winter's night, with snow drifting beneath the eaves, there is no finer dish to warm the soul than beef bourguignon. Tender beef simmered in good red wine with onions, bacon, mushrooms, and herbs, it is French comfort food at its best. At its heart, this is just a beef stew. And stew is simple, so I make it simply. Brown, deglaze, and braise—that's all there really is to it.

INGREDIENTS:

1½ lbs. chuck roast cut into 1" cubes
½ lb. crimini mushrooms, quartered
½ lb. bacon, cut into ½" lardons
½ lb. carrots, sliced into ¾" rounds
1 medium yellow onion, diced
5 cloves garlic, finely diced
½ lb. pearl onions, peeled
2 tbsp flour
4 oz. tomato paste
2 cups beef broth
2 cups red wine (preferably pinot noir or burgundy)
1 tbsp fresh thyme leaves, finely chopped
2 tbsp parsley, finely chopped

DIRECTIONS:

In a large, heavy-bottomed pot, cook the bacon pieces over medium heat until it is crisp and the fat is rendered. Remove the bacon to a plate while retaining the fat in the pot.

Add the beef cubes, season with salt and pepper, and sear them until they are browned on all sides. Then remove them to the plate with the bacon.

Next add the carrots, garlic, and diced onion to the pot and cook until the onions are translucent. Add the 2 tbsp flour and stir to coat the vegetables. Cook this for 2 minutes, or until the flour begins to stick to the bottom and brown. Then add the tomato paste and cook for 2 additional minutes.

Add the wine and broth to the pot and scrape the bottom to remove the fond. Return the beef and bacon to the pot and add the mushrooms, pearl onions, bay leaves, thyme, and parsley.

Bring to a boil, then reduce heat to low, cover, and simmer for 1 hour. After 1 hour, remove the lid and simmer for an additional 15 minutes to allow some moisture to cook off.

Taste, and add salt if desired. Serve over egg noodles with nice, crusty bread.

MOUSSE THREE WAYS

When it comes to making desserts in a tiny kitchen, or even in a campground, there are few better options than mousse. It is light and airy, but also rich and decadent. And, as it turns out, it's really easy to make just about anywhere. In fact, it's so simple that I think you ought to go ahead and make three flavors at once and assemble yourself a gorgeous parfait.

INGREDIENTS:

Chocolate Mousse:
1 cup heavy cream
6 oz. chocolate of your choice (I prefer a medium cacao dark chocolate)

Vanilla Mousse:
1 cup heavy whipping cream
2 tsp powdered sugar
¼ tsp vanilla extract

Strawberry Mousse:
1¾ cups strawberries
¼ cup sugar
1 cup heavy cream

DIRECTIONS:

Chocolate Mousse:
Melt the chocolate in a pan over low heat. Whip the cream until it holds stiff peaks. Fold in the melted chocolate.

Vanilla Mousse:
Add the cream, sugar, and vanilla to a mixing bowl and whisk until the whipped cream is nice and thick, and holds a peak.

Strawberry Mousse:
Puree the strawberries and sugar in a food processor (or mash by hand). Whip the cream until it holds stiff peaks. Fold in the strawberry puree, reserving ½ cup. Serve by putting a healthy smear of strawberry puree around the bottom of each serving dish and then covering it with strawberry mousse.

If you're feeling ambitious, make all three flavors and stack the chocolate and vanilla on top of the strawberry and finish with sliced straverries and shaved chocolate.

BUILDING OUR BUS

Many of you holding this book are probably wondering how the hell we ended up living in an old school bus and traveling the country. And those of you for whom that already makes perfect sense are probably more curious about the specifics of our build. This interlude is for all of you. I'll tell you a bit about us, how we ended up buying a bus together, and what it's like in there.

It's kind of a funny story actually, how it all began. A mutual friend set Ayana and I up for a casual date, as we were both recently out of big relationships and not looking for anything too serious, and we met for a cocktail in a basement bar. It was the fourth of July, so after the first drink awkwardness was out of the way, we grabbed a bottle of champagne and climbed into the hills above Boulder to watch the fireworks.

In between booming explosions and flashes of brilliant color, we shared stories of where we'd traveled, the places we dreamed of visiting, and all the other things that set our souls on fire. At some point in the night, Ayana looked me in the eye and asked, "Do you want to live in a van?"

I wasn't sure if she was asking if I wanted to live in a van with her, or if our friend had just let on that I was headed down that dirtbag path, but hearing that question from such a beautiful woman left me without words. Instead of answering the question, I kissed her.

Fast forward a few months and we were elbow-deep in the classifieds searching for our rig. We had looked at a few possibilities: a standard, white cargo van; a small, rickety, half-built Air Force van; and one rusty, old, party bus; but none of them were right. They were all either too expensive for our tiny budget, too run down, or too small for the two of us and a puggle. On a whim, Ayana sent a message to a van-builder in Denver asking if he had anything we might like. He got back to us quickly and invited us down to check out the extra rig one of his employees just happened to have on the lot at the time.

We first laid eyes on our Sweet Bea in a barren industrial yard practically underneath I-70. She

definitely needed some work, but the price was right, and the size felt good. Ayana gave her a test drive, and we headed home, still unsure if she was the right choice.

The hemming and hawing continued for a few days, as we weighed the pros and cons. She was very cheap, but probably needed some mechanical work, and the maintenance on an old rig was likely to be frequent and expensive. The size was good, but we weren't sure that we wanted to take on a project that required so much demolition when we could just buy a cargo van and get straight to building. We really couldn't make up our minds. And then I spotted what I took to be an omen. Somehow I'd missed it during our first meeting, but emblazoned right on the side of her was Ayana's and my shared lucky number: 22. I typically think of myself as a logic-driven person,

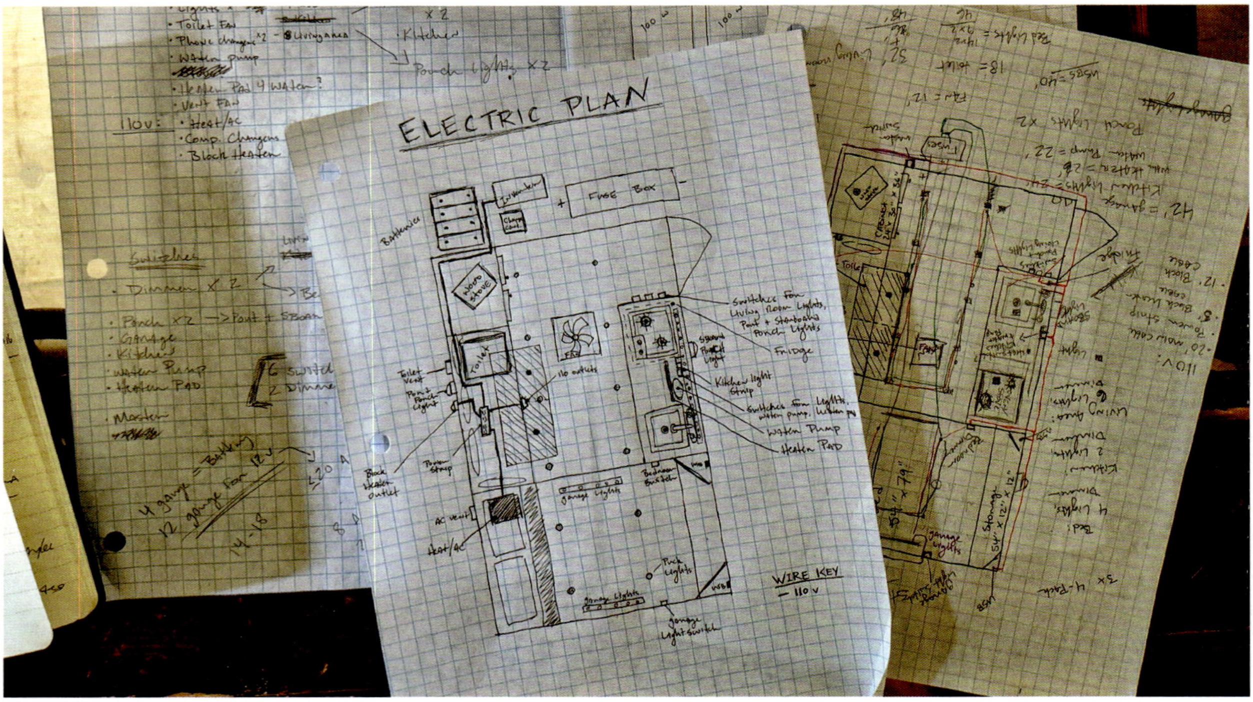

not so susceptible to superstition, but how could it not be a good sign that Bea's fleet number happened to be the one number that was so significant to both of us? In this instance, that little slice of superstition was exactly what we needed to push us over the line (that and the good price). On October 28th, 2018, after knowing each other for less than four months, we brought our Sweet Bea home.

The day we brought the bus home was certainly wonderful, but it was a day that Ayana and I learned that our approaches to this project were quite different from one another. It was a gorgeous autumn afternoon when that rickety, old bus rolled up to Boulder. We parked her on the street outside my apartment, popped a bottle of champagne, and sat inside on the bare floor, dreaming about what we could build. We felt like kids in a clubhouse, sitting in that empty bus with the leaves fluttering outside the window. But, as we dreamed of this and that, of a wood stove and a roof deck, of a big kitchen and a queen-sized bed, I could feel my stress levels rising. Ayana could see all of the amazing things that we could build, and with each new idea I was struck by the same thought: I don't have any idea how the fuck we do that. Neither of us had any experience with building, and I was beginning to feel that we might have bitten off more than we could chew.

It wasn't until January that we really got started on the build. There were some mechanical issues that needed to be worked out, and we were both busy with the holidays. But also, if I'm being honest, we were both pretty intimidated by the project. Neither of us really knew where to start.

Fortunately, that's when we met Mike.

Ayana found us a weekend workshop nearby at a place called Satsang Vanworks. While the class was not perfect and led us into a few dead-ends with regard to electrical work, it gave us a desperately-needed toehold that we could start from. It also gave us the name of a professional that we could call when we needed someone to check our work or take over when we got in too deep.

In total, the build took us about 18 months. We were both working full-time, so it was a project of weekends, but honestly I don't know that we could have learned all of those skills any faster. Every task in a van or bus build requires learning a new skill, and most of the time, when you finish a task, you put that skill on the shelf and never touch it again. If we were to build another one, we would be done

in 6 months, but those hours we spent watching youtube videos and scouring the internet to learn the myriad skills of a plumber, electrician, and carpenter (among others), added up quickly.

Throughout the process we were incredibly thankful for Mike's help. He double-checked our electrical plans, helped install our windows, pointed us to a good contractor for our spray foam, gave a stamp of approval on our deck, and, when we needed to speed things up, he took over the cabinetry for us. We might have been able to do it all without his help, but it would have taken us much, much longer. This isn't the acknowledgements section, so I'll call it there with the thank yous, but we did receive help from many hands along the way, and we are very thankful to every one of them.

It was a long year and a half of work, with more than a few challenges and squabbles, but the day did eventually come when Bea was ready for the road. We held our buswarming party, one of my all-time happiest memories, where hundreds of our friends and family showed up to drink a beer with us in our new home. Unfortunately, after the party and right on the eve of our departure, a now infamous little coronavirus showed up and pushed it all back. Our first six months in the bus happened in a Boulder driveway (memories for another book), but we did eventually hit the road full-time, and we haven't looked back since.

But enough narrative, tell us what's in the damn thing! Alright, alright, for you technically-minded folks out there, here are some of the specs from our build. Excluding the cab, she has about 90 square feet of living space (7.5' x 12'). In that space we put a queen bed, a 5' couch with a swiveling takedown table, a hideaway composting toilet, and a tiny wood-burning stove. The kitchen has a 3-burner propane cooktop, a sink with no hot water, and a 70-liter fridge. Nearly every other bit of space in the bus was dedicated to storage of some kind.

One of the more unique features of our skoolie is the second seat up front. The classic bus doors typically preclude a passenger seat, as it would fall smack dab in the middle of the walkway. We were able to solve this problem with the help of a welder friend, who closed up those big, glass doors for us and cut down our handicap door to a standard 30" width. We then climbed up underneath the bus and bolt a swiveling captain's chair with a second seatbelt into that newly created space.

As for our daily resources, we run everything off of our battery bank, which is charged by the solar array on top of the bus. We have 300 amp hours of lithium batteries and 300-watts of solar panels. We have a water tank under the bed that holds around 18 gallons, and we carry an additional 13 gallons in jerry cans, for when we need a refill. That quantity of water will typically last us about 10 days in the desert. We do carry a propane-powered generator for back-up power when the solar can't keep up, and there is a heater/AC unit under the bed for climate control when we have access to shore power. If you want more details, you can find all the nitty gritty on our websites.

And that, my friends, is about all there is to it. We met, fell in love, and bought a bus startlingly, recklessly quickly, but we also both knew from the very beginning that this person was different. Our intuitions, it seems, were impressively accurate, and three and a half years later, as I'm writing this, we're still madly in love and as happy as ever that we chose to make that madcap leap together. Building your dream home into a tiny, old bus with your partner will certainly test your relationship at times, but for us it turned out to be exactly the right choice, and it has taken us to just where we want to be.

BRUNCH RECIPES

TRIPLE CHOCOLATE PANCAKES WITH COFFEE MOUSSE

This recipe is about as decadent as it gets: chocolate pancakes with walnuts and chocolate chips, covered in chocolate syrup and a dollop of mousse. Sounds freaking good, right? This was one of those recipes that popped into my head and then I just HAD to make it.

INGREDIENTS:

Pancakes:

1⅓ cups flour
¼ cup cocoa powder
¼ cup sugar
¼ tsp salt
2 tsp baking powder
1 cup milk
2 eggs, beaten
2 tbsp neutral oil
1 tsp vanilla extract
¼ cup walnuts
¼ cup chocolate chips
Chocolate syrup, to taste

Mousse:

1 cup heavy whipping cream
1 tbsp + 1 tsp instant espresso powder
1 tbsp sugar

DIRECTIONS:

Pancakes:

In a large bowl, mix together the flour, cocoa powder, sugar, salt, and baking powder. In a separate bowl, beat the eggs and then beat in the milk, oil, and vanilla extract. Add the wet ingredients to the dry ingredients and stir together until a nice batter is formed.

Heat a skillet over medium heat and add some butter or oil. Ladle out ¼ cup of batter into the center. Sprinkle over some chocolate chips and walnuts. When the first bubbles form in the center of the pancake, flip it, and cook for 1 minute on the other side.

Mousse:

Add 1 cup cold heavy whipping cream, 1 tbsp sugar, and 1 tbsp + 1 tsp instant espresso powder to a mixing bowl. Beat the mixture with an electric whisk until it is nice and thick and holds peaks.

To serve:

Stack the pancakes to desired height, drizzle with chocolate syrup, and top with a nice dollop of coffee mousse. Allow the pancakes to cool before adding the mousse or it will melt off.

BISCUITS WITH MUSHROOM AND ONION GRAVY

Biscuits and gravy is my favorite breakfast. While traditionally country gravy is made with breakfast sausage, in this recipe the gravy is flavored with onions and mushrooms as well as a bit of sage and garlic. With ingredients like that, you won't miss the meat at all. The mushrooms lend umami and texture, the onions a touch of sweetness, and the garlic, sage, and black pepper round out the flavor for a truly rich vegetarian country gravy. Put this on your next Sunday brunch menu.

INGREDIENTS:

Biscuits:
4 cups flour
2 tbsp baking powder
1 stick butter
2 tsp salt
1 ½ cups milk

Gravy:
3 tbsp butter
1 medium yellow onion, diced
8 oz. mushrooms, diced
3 cloves garlic, minced
2 tsp dried sage
2 tsp black pepper
3 tbsp flour
3 cups milk
2 tsp apple cider vinegar

DIRECTIONS:

Biscuits:
See biscuit recipe on page 55.

Gravy:
Melt the butter in a large skillet over medium heat. Add the onions, garlic, and mushrooms, and cook until onions are translucent. Add the spices and flour and cook, stirring occasionally, for a few minutes, until the flour begins to brown and crisp on the edges of the mushroom and onion pieces.

Add the milk slowly, about a half cup at a time, stirring all the while. When all the milk has been added, cook it down to your desired thickness, remembering that it will thicken slightly as it cools.

If the gravy is too thick, you can add a bit more milk. If it is too thin, let it reduce for a little while.

Mix in the cider vinegar and salt to taste. Serve over fresh biscuits, and alongside a couple of fried eggs.

These breakfast tacos are easy to put together and perfect for tailgating before the chairlift or cooking at camp before a big hike. All you need is cheesy eggs, corn tortillas, and a killer fresh salsa (which you can make the night before) to pack a punch of flavor in there. If you want to add a bit of bacon or sausage, it definitely won't hurt things. And feel free to deck it out with sour cream, hot sauce, et cetera. Makes about 8 tacos.

INGREDIENTS:

8 eggs
8 corn tortillas
½ cup sharp cheddar cheese
¼ cup white onion, minced
¼ cup green pepper, minced
¼ cup red pepper, finely minced
1 jalapeno, finely minced
¼ tsp cumin
¼ tsp chili powder
Juice of ½ lime

DIRECTIONS:

Salsa:
Mince the onion, jalapenos, and bell peppers. Add the cumin, chili powder, and lime juice. Make this first so it has a little while to sit and incorporate. Making it a day ahead won't hurt it one bit.

Tacos:
Soft scramble the eggs over medium heat, stirring often (about 1 per taco). When the eggs are about half cooked, add half the cheese and stir to incorporate. Remove the eggs from heat while still moist and put them on warm corn tortillas.

To warm the tortillas, cook them briefly in a hot skillet or directly over the flame of a burner. This chars them slightly and keeps them from breaking when wrapped around those delicious fillings.

Top with the remaining cheese and finish with the pepper salsa, your desired hot sauce, and sour cream.

ORANGE FRENCH TOAST

French toast is a wonderful dish for a home brunch, transforming a stale loaf of bread into a custardy delight. And, while a coating of maple syrup is a perfectly wonderful way to dress it up, French toast takes on a whole new level of elegance when infused with the delicate flavors and aromas of freshly-squeezed orange juice. All it takes is a few large oranges and a little bit of powdered sugar, and that standard Sunday brunch meal turns into something altogether new and exciting.

INGREDIENTS:

½ loaf french bread
4 eggs, beaten
2 tbsp half and half
½ cup freshly squeezed orange juice (buy ~3-4 large oranges total)
¼ tsp vanilla extract

Toppings:
Butter
Powdered Sugar
¼ cup freshly squeezed orange juice
1 orange, thinly sliced

DIRECTIONS:

Beat the eggs in a bowl and add milk, freshly squeezed orange juice, and vanilla extract. Beat this together until uniform. Reserve ¼ cup orange juice as well as 1 orange for topping.

Slice the French bread into 1" thick pieces and dip them in the batter, allowing them time to soak it up on either side.

Heat a skillet over medium heat and add butter. When hot, add the soaked bread and cook until nicely browned on both sides.

Cut the peel from the remaining orange and slice it into small pieces. In a bowl, combine ¼ cup freshly squeezed orange juice, the orange pieces, and powdered sugar to taste. Stir this together, taste, and adjust as necessary.

To serve, spread each piece with a bit of butter, top it with a spoon or two of the orange syrup, and sprinkle with a bit of additional powdered sugar.

THE PERFECT BREAKFAST BURRITO

The days of oatmeal have passed. The breakfast burrito is the new backbone of modern adventure food. Who wants to eat a bowl of bland gruel, when they could just pop their campstove on the tailgate long enough to fry a couple eggs and wrap it all up in a tortilla? Whether it's cooking at the trailhead before a big hike or the parking lot before grabbing first chair, a breakfast burrito is the way to go. This recipe is a little complicated, but if you prep a few things ahead of time, it will be no trouble at all. Makes 2 good-sized burritos.

INGREDIENTS:

4 eggs
¼ cup roasted green chiles
¼ cup red enchilada sauce
1 cup tater tots
¼ cup black beans
½ cup shredded cheese of your choice
2 large flour tortillas

DIRECTIONS:

The tater tots take the longest, so they should be done first. If you have an oven, feel free to bake them, but they are tastier if you fry them. You can pan fry them pretty quickly, just add a bit of oil to a skillet over medium-high heat and fry until golden brown, flipping as necessary to get them cooked on both sides. When they are done, scoop them out onto a plate with a paper towel to collect excess oil and salt liberally.

Soft scramble your eggs over medium-low heat. When they are about halfway cooked, add half the shredded cheese (¼ cup) and mix together well. Remove from heat before your eggs are cooked hard (unless you like that kind of thing).

Once those things are cooked, mix everything together and split it evenly between your two tortillas. Warming your tortilla a bit can help with wrapping this hefty burrito. If you want things spicier, add a little hot sauce to the mix before you wrap it up to keep the mess down. But a little extra hot sauce never hurt anyone, so keep that on hand when serving as well.

EGGS BENEDICT TWO WAYS

Hollandaise sauce has a reputation for being quite finicky and can be intimidating for those who have never made it before. Fortunately, it is actually deceptively simple. Those eggs benedict that you've been paying so much for at Sunday brunch can be whipped up in no time. Seriously, throw in a couple bottles of champagne and orange juice, and you've got yourself an amazing brunch that won't cost you $50 a head.

INGREDIENTS:

Hollandaise Sauce:
½ lb. butter
3 egg yolks + 1 whole egg
¼ cup white wine vinegar
Squeeze of Fresh Lemon Juice
Sprinkle of cayenne
Salt, to taste

Benedict (per serving):
2 eggs
1 english muffin
2 slices canadian bacon
Hollandaise sauce

Cali Benny (per serving):
2 eggs
1 english muffin
2 large slices tomato
½ avocado, sliced
Hollandaise sauce

DIRECTIONS:

Hollandaise Sauce:
Beat together egg, yolks, and vinegar until uniform in a heat-safe bowl. Place this bowl over a medium-heat bain marie and whisk until the mixture just begins to thicken. Begin adding melted butter in small increments, totalling 4 or 5 additions. Once all butter is whisked in and sauce reaches desired consistency, remove from heat.

Add a sprinkle of cayenne and a squeeze of fresh lemon juice, and whisk these in. Taste, and adjust seasoning as desired with salt, cayenne, lemon, etc.

Toast the english muffins and put two halves on each plate. Top with either a warmed slice of canadian bacon, or a lightly salted slice of tomato and several avocado slices.

Bring a saucepan of water to a gentle boil on the stove. Crack an egg into a large spoon or ladle, and gently lower it into the boiling water. Cook each egg for 2.5-3 minutes, and then scoop it out with a slotted spoon. To check the eggs, simply lift them to the surface with your slotted spoon, it should be easy to see when the whites are cooked and the yolk is still runny.

When scooping the poached eggs out, carefully tilt the slotted spoon to drain the water from the eggs to keep from wetting your english muffins. Place one poached egg on each muffin, and finish with a hefty drizzle of hollandaise.

BISCUITS WITH GREEN CHILE CHORIZO GRAVY

Given how much I like to play when I'm cooking, we have tried a lot of different varieties of biscuits and gravy. There are even two different recipes in this dang cookbook alone, this one and a vegetarian variety made with onions and mushrooms. This recipe, made with chorizo and green chile, definitely takes the cake. It is the best damn country gravy I've ever had, absolutely to die for poured over some hot biscuits. But also try putting it on hashbrowns or in a breakfast burrito while you're at it, you won't be disappointed.

INGREDIENTS:

Biscuits:
4 cups flour
2 tbsp baking powder
1 stick butter
2 tsp salt
1 ½ cups milk

Gravy:
9 oz. Mexican chorizo
½ cup green chile
3 tbsp flour
3 cups milk
1 tsp white vinegar
1 tsp cumin
Salt, to taste

DIRECTIONS:

Biscuits:
See biscuit recipe on page 55

Gravy:
Begin by cooking the sausage over medium heat in a large saucepan. Break it apart and cook until the meat is cooked through and the fat rendered. Then add the spices and 3 tbsp flour to the meat and mix well to combine. Allow this to cook for a few minutes to get rid of the raw flour taste.

Begin adding the milk around ½ cup at a time, stirring each time until the consistency is even throughout the pan. Continue adding milk until all 3 cups are in the pan. Then add your green chiles.

Now reduce the gravy to your desired consistency over medium heat. Remember, it will thicken slightly once it is removed from heat. When you reach your desired consistency, add 1 tsp white vinegar and salt to taste.

SHAKSHUKA WITH GOAT CHEESE

Shakshuka is a dish of eggs poached in a sauce of tomato, pepper, onion, and fresh herbs. It originated in northern Africa in the time of the Ottoman empire, and has since become popular in the middle-east and really all over the world. It is a wonderful dish for breakfast, lunch, or dinner, and it is also perfect for vanlife. Not only is it an inexpensive and healthy meal (both high on the list for most vanlifers), it is also all cooked in just one pot. Any meal that can be made in a single dish is great for those of us who like to boondock out in places where we have limited water. The fewer dishes you need to wash, the longer you can stay out there. And having some good bread on hand will make things even easier, as you will want to sop up every drop of that sauce.

INGREDIENTS:

1 medium yellow onion, diced
1 red bell pepper, diced
1 green bell pepper, diced
4 cloves garlic, minced
2 tbsp tomato paste
2 cups crushed tomato
2 tsp cumin
1 tsp red pepper flakes (optional)
½ tsp smoked paprika
¼ tsp nutmeg
¼ cup chopped parsley
¼ cup chopped cilantro
½ cup crumbled goat cheese
6 eggs
Salt + Pepper, to taste

DIRECTIONS:

Char the diced bell peppers and onions with a small amount of oil in a large skillet with lid over medium-high heat. When they are charred at the edges, reduce the heat to medium and add the tomato paste and garlic. Stir together and cook for around 3 minutes, until slightly darkened.

Add the 2 cups of crushed tomato, spices, and herbs. Stir together, scrape the bottom, and simmer for 10 minutes. Add the goat cheese. Adjust the seasoning of the sauce with additional salt and spices, if desired.

Make wells for the eggs in the sauce, and add them. Cover the pan and allow the eggs to steam for a few minutes. When they are white on top, they should be perfect—cooked through, but still soft with beautifully runny yolks.

Serve with bread or toast to dip in the sauce. Also great with tortilla chips.

THAI RECIPES

THAI BEEF SALAD

Thai beef salad is, in many ways, a perfect appetizer. It has thin slices of grilled beef resting on a bed of tomatoes, cucumbers, and fresh herbs, all rounded out with a spicy, complex, and explosively flavorful dressing. Padded out with a bit of additional lettuce, this amazing starter easily becomes a meal all on its own.

INGREDIENTS:

1 lb. ribeye, flat-iron, or skirt steak
1 lb. cherry tomatoes, halved
2 cucumbers, peeled, seeded, and chopped
½ cup green onions, thinly sliced
¼ cup mint, finely chopped
¼ cup cilantro, finely chopped
½ serrano, finely chopped (optional)

Dressing:
1 clove garlic, minced
1 jalapeno, seeded and minced
Juice of 1 lime
2 tbsp fish sauce
2 tbsp lemongrass paste
1 tbsp sugar
¼ cup shallot, minced

DIRECTIONS:

Mix all the dressing ingredients together in a small bowl and allow the flavors to meld for at least 30 minutes.

Chop and mix together all the salad ingredients in a large bowl. Pour over the dressing and mix to coat all the vegetables. Set this aside while you grill your beef on a fire, grill pan, or cast iron.

Season the steak with salt and pepper and grill for a few minutes on each side to achieve a nice sear and a rare cook. Rest the meat and slice it into ¼ inch slices.

To plate, lay a few slices of beef over a generous couple scoops of salad.

CHICKEN SATAY

Many of the best known (and tastiest) Thai dishes are street food. Things like pad thai, papaya salad, mango sticky rice, and this beautiful chicken satay, can be bought on the corner from an expert chef who often sells only their specialty. You know that the guy who makes his living selling only one dish must make a pretty mean satay. I don't claim that this recipe is on the level of those experts, but I will tell you that dipped in peanut sauce and paired with a couple of cold lagers, these go down just as well as the real thing. If you close your eyes, you might be able, just for a second, to hear the tuk-tuks whizzing past.

INGREDIENTS:

1½ lbs. Chicken thighs, sliced to 1" cubes
Marinade:
½ cup coconut milk
¼ white onion, sliced thinly
2 tbsp lemongrass paste
2 tbsp garlic, minced
2 tbsp ginger, minced
2 tbsp brown sugar
2 tbsp soy sauce
2 tbsp fish sauce
2 tbsp red curry paste
1 serrano, sliced thinly
Peanut Sauce:
2 tbsp red curry paste
¾ cup natural peanut butter
¼ cup sugar
1 tsp sesame oil
Juice of 1 lime
2 tsp soy sauce
2 tbsp white vinegar
¾ cup water
Salt, to taste

DIRECTIONS:

Mix together the marinade ingredients. Add the cubed chicken thighs and allow to marinate for 2 hours or more. During this time you should also soak your bamboo skewers in a bit of water to keep them from catching fire on the grill.

In a small saucepan, combine the peanut sauce ingredients and simmer, stirring occasionally, until smooth and uniform. Adjust seasonings as desired. This will produce more peanut sauce than you need, but it can be stored in the fridge for quite a while or used as a great sauce for spicy Thai pizza.

Fill the bamboo skewers with chicken pieces and grill them on a medium-hot grill or grill pan until cooked through and browned on the outside.

Serve with peanut sauce and a few cold lagers.

PANANG CURRY FISH

Panang curry is my go-to whenever we order Thai food. It is spicy, rich, and slightly sweet, which really does it for me. But for years whenever I tried to make panang (or any other) Thai curry at home, which we often do, I was disappointed in the results. It was just never as flavorful as what I got from the restaurant. It took many rounds of pretty-good-but-not-great curry until I finally figured out the missing pieces. I am happy to share that with just a few simple additions, you can take your homemade Thai curry up to restaurant quality.

INGREDIENTS:

1 yellow onion cut to eighths and sliced thin
1 green bell pepper, sliced thin
1 red bell pepper, sliced thin
2 carrots, sliced thin
2 cloves garlic, minced
2 tbsp panang curry paste
1 can coconut milk
½ cup water
2 kaffir lime leaves
1½ lb. fish fillets (tilapia, swai, cod, salmon, whatever really)

Finish with:
2 tbsp peanut butter
1 tbsp fish sauce
1½ tsp sugar
2 tsp lime juice
2 tbsp basil, finely chopped

DIRECTIONS:

Saute vegetables over medium heat until somewhat softened and fragrant. Add the curry paste and kaffir lime leaves, stir together, and allow to cook for another 2 minutes. Add the coconut milk, water, cover, and reduce heat to medium-low. Simmer for around 10 minutes, or until carrots are softened.

Uncover, add the fish filets, and poach them for a few minutes until they are just cooked.

Remove the curry from heat and add the fish sauce, sugar, peanut butter, lime juice, and basil. Stir together well and allow to cool for a few minutes before serving.

Serve over rice.

Som Tam, which translates literally to "pounded sour," is a broad term referring to the sweet, sour, salty, and spicy green papaya salads popular in Thailand. Traditionally, this dish is made in a clay mortar and pounded with a wooden pestle, using whatever vegetables are abundant at the time. The ingredients are added bit by bit and pounded until they are just right. For the home cook, a food processor and a grater or julienne will do the job.

INGREDIENTS:

2½ cups green papaya (from ~3 lb. fruit), grated large
2 cloves garlic
1 serrano chili
1 tbsp brown sugar
1 tsp neutral oil
2 tbsp dried shrimp (optional)
½ cup peanuts
¾ cup cherry tomatoes, halved
2 tbsp fish sauce
3 tbsp lime juice

DIRECTIONS:

Traditionally, this dish would be made in a mortar and pestle, but fortunately a food processor also does the job quite well.

Add the garlic cloves, chilies, 1 tbsp brown sugar, and 1 tsp neutral oil to your food processor and blend to a paste. If you are sensitive to heat, consider seeding the serrano before use. Personally, I prefer this dish to be quite spicy.

Add the dried shrimp, if you are using them, and blend until they are a part of the paste. Add the peanuts to the food processor and pulse until they are nicely chopped. Add the fish sauce and lime juice to the food processor and pulse a few times to mix.

Grate your papaya with the largest grater you have. Try to get as much unripe papaya as you can, while avoiding the more ripe, orangey parts.

Put the grated papaya in a mixing bowl and dress with the sauce from the food processor. Add the halved cherry tomatoes and toss.

Garnish with chopped cilantro and additional chopped peanuts.

Pad Thai often serves as an introduction to Thai food for the wary eater. Those who fear to dive straight into a bowl of spicy curry can instead dip their toes daintily into the waters of a more familiar, less spicy, and still wonderfully delicious, plate of stir-fried noodles. For this reason, pad Thai has become something of a global ambassador for Thai culture and a widely recognized symbol of Thailand. And as it turns out, it was actually created specifically to be the Thai national dish.

INGREDIENTS:

8 oz. rice noodles, linguini-sized
¾ lb. small shrimp, peeled
½ lb. extra firm tofu, sliced into bite-size pieces
2 eggs, beaten
3 tbsp brown sugar (or palm sugar)
3 tbsp tamarind paste
4 tbsp fish sauce
2 tbsp fresh lime juice
2 medium shallots, finely diced
6 cloves garlic, minced
6 scallions, thinly sliced
3 tbsp peanuts, chopped
1 cup bean sprouts

DIRECTIONS:

Begin by soaking the rice noodles in cold water for one hour. By the end, they should be pliable but firm. Drain the noodles.

In a bowl, combine the tamarind paste, fish sauce, lime juice, and brown (or palm) sugar. Stir to dissolve the sugar and set aside.

Add 2 tablespoons of high-heat oil to a large skillet or wok over medium-high heat. Once hot, add the noodles and stir fry for 1 minute. Pour the bowl of sauce over the noodles and stir to ensure that they are all nicely coated. Reduce the heat to medium and push the noodles to one side of the pan.

On the other side of the pan, add a bit of oil and then the shallots, garlic, shrimp, and tofu. Allow these to fry until the shrimp are mostly cooked, stirring occasionally. Also be sure to mix up the noodles every once in a while to keep them from sticking or burning on the bottom.

Mix everything in the pan together and then push it to the outside, creating a well in the center. Pour the beaten eggs into the well and scramble them there. Your noodles should be cooked through. If not, you can now add a bit of water and saute them until they are tender.

When the eggs are done, remove the pan from heat, mix in 1 cup of bean sprouts, and allow them to wilt slightly. Dish out your servings and top with sliced scallions and chopped peanuts.

Serve with limes, fish sauce, sriracha, and additional bean sprouts.

Quick, simple, and delicious, mango sticky rice (khao niew ma muang) is one of the finest desserts not only in Thailand, but the world over. It is as simple as cooking rice, whipping up a quick sauce of sugar and coconut cream, and topping it with a bit of sliced mango. It is also one of Ayana's favorite desserts. When she was in Thailand, on the island of Kho Yao Noi, she would go back each morning to the pier, to the same lady, to buy one of these glorious little banana leaf-wrapped packets of joy and eat her breakfast while the tide rolled in. For the sake of ease we forego the banana leaf steaming and often use jasmine rice, but they are best made with Thai glutinous rice, as it is slightly sweeter and stickier.

INGREDIENTS:

1 cup jasmine rice (or Thai glutinous rice)
1½ cups water
1½ cups coconut cream
½ cup sugar
½ tsp salt
2 tsp rice flour
2 tbsp toasted sesame seeds
2 mangos, sliced thin

DIRECTIONS:

Begin by cooking the rice. If you struggle to cook rice on the stove, here is the foolproof method: add rice and water to a small saucepan with a lid and bring to a boil over medium-high heat. When the rice reaches a good boil, turn the heat down to low and simmer covered for 10 minutes. After simmering, remove the saucepan from heat and allow to steam covered for 10 additional minutes. When you open the lid after the 10 minutes of steaming, you should have a pot of perfectly cooked rice.

In another saucepan, make the sauce by combining the coconut cream (scoop the solids from the top of a can of coconut milk), salt, rice flour, and sugar. Stir this over medium-low heat until it is hot and well-combined.

Add the rice to the sauce, and mix together until evenly distributed. It can be served warm or cool, depending on preference. The mixture will thicken as it cools, so it is also a question of preferred texture.

Serve topped with toasted sesame seeds and thinly sliced mango.

THAI TEA PUDDING

This recipe brings the unique flavor of Thai tea to a dessert which is simultaneously familiar and exotic, and is also easy to make ahead and have waiting in the fridge to cap off an amazing meal. Grab a bag of Thai tea mix from your local Asian grocer, and you're already half-way to this wonderful dessert.

INGREDIENTS:

3 cups milk
¼ cup thai tea mix
¼ cup sugar
¼ cup corn starch
2 tbsp butter
A pinch of salt

DIRECTIONS:

Make a steeping bag out of cheesecloth for the ¼ cup of tea mix, or put it in a device made for steeping loose tea. Simmer 2½ cups of milk with sugar and tea mix in a saucepan over medium-low heat for 6-8 minutes, until the tea is nicely steeped. Do not boil. Remove from heat and discard the tea.

In a small bowl, mix ¼ cup cornstarch and ½ cup of cold milk. Stir to mix well.

Test the temperature of the tea-steeped milk. Cornstarch cooks at around 165 degrees, so the mixture must be below that temperature before you mix in the cornstarch.

Pour the cornstarch slurry into the pot with the steeped milk, whisk well, and then return it to the stove over low heat. Cook the mixture, stirring constantly, and watching the temperature. At around 165 degrees it will begin to thicken, becoming quite cooked by 170. At this point, remove it from heat. If you don't have a thermometer, you can tell the pudding is cooked when it is suddenly thick enough to coat the back of a spoon.

Add the 2 tablespoons of butter and pinch of salt. Stir together until the butter is melted and mixed in. Pour the pudding into individual serving vessels if desired, or into a large serving bowl. Put this in the refrigerator for at least a couple hours to cool and set. A piece of plastic wrap on the surface will prevent a skin forming.

IT'S ONLY FOOD

For as long as I've been tall enough to reach the stovetop, I have loved to cook. The men in my family were all accomplished in the kitchen, and my father and older brothers shared that with me from an early age. When I was so young that the only recipe in my repertoire was bacon and eggs, I was always eager to cook up a batch for whatever friends were over, mine or not, whether it was Sunday morning or Friday midnight. Serving good food to hungry people has been a lifelong pleasure for me.

Until I met Ayana, I kind of thought everyone was that way. I was completely unaware that there was an entire section of society that simply does not like to cook. Up to that point, I think that every person I had ever known had at least some dish that they enjoyed preparing. But for Ayana that just wasn't the case. She is more than capable in the kitchen, and has never served me anything that wasn't great, but for her the whole process, from the grocery store to the dinner table, is stressful, and she'd rather leave it to the professionals at the local takeout restaurant (or me).

Now, I would guess that most people reading this book probably enjoy cooking a bit more than that. You have, after all, already picked up a cookbook and dedicated some time to reading it. But I know that there are probably a few folks out there that are flipping through thinking that these recipes are too damn complicated. I assure you, cooking is much easier than it is often made out to be. I hope that this essay will make the whole process seem a little bit less intimidating.

I am going to start with what I think is the biggest problem out there right now: Gordon-fucking-Ramsay (as his ilk). This man made a career out of taking the most over-the-top machismo of the biggest assholes in the culinary world and turning it toward home cooks and struggling restaurant owners. The pretentious attitude of people like him is completely unnecessary in the world of food (at least outside of a Michelin-starred kitchen), and the growing popularity of competitive cooking shows means that too many of us have watched him throw down his fork in fury, or spit into a napkin as if he'd been served a dish straight from the litterbox, all because

the protein was slightly underdone or it was a little bit too spicy for him. I worked as a wildland firefighter for years, and was always put off by the level of machismo exhibited there, but I can tell you that even in that situation, when people's lives were actually on the line, no one held a candle to Gordon Ramsay. Bringing that level of drama to a plate of dumplings is nothing short of foolish to me. And that attitude definitely doesn't belong in the home kitchen.

When you're cooking, if your protein is a little under-done, just throw it back on the heat. If your gravy is lumpy, strain it, or just enjoy it lumpy. If you oversalt the sauce, you can thin it out or use less of it. Very rarely does one of these minor foibles ruin or even really damage a meal. It will definitely still be delicious.

In addition to the artificially high stakes of cooking, there is a tendency in the culinary world to create rules and secret tricks, most of which are hogwash. I often see recipes, particularly on the internet, with long lists of dos and don'ts, most of which are completely unnecessary. People, especially people on the internet desperate for you to look at their website, love to create a prob-

lem so that they can solve it for you. Every one of these online chefs is trying to bait you to their website by promising some sacred culinary roadmap to the perfect pasta carbonara. When you get there, unable to resist the temptation to see if they have actually uncovered an ancient text from the fabled pyramid of parmigiano, what you find is typically a series of very specific instructions that I would guess they have never actually tested themselves. Whether it is the perfect number of stirs or the exact salinity of the pasta water, most of these people are probably not producing good-quality science here. In reality, most dishes out there, save for a finicky few, are actually pretty easy. It really is just food, and it's not that complicated.

Beyond the dubious lists of culinary pitfalls, there are also many questionable rules that even chefs at the highest level often tout. Cooking is an art with plenty of principles, and few real rules, but that does not prevent these chefs from regularly referring to them. Cuts of meat with high levels of collagen are best when cooked slowly to allow the collagen to dissolve and create a perfect, unctuous bite. That is a principle based in measurable, repeatable, science. That same piece of meat with a quick sear would be tough and unpleasant. A rule, on the other hand, falls into the

dogma side of cooking, and as much as chefs on tv and in media might repeat them, they are broken again and again. If I have to hear one more famous chef say nervously that seafood and dairy should never be mixed, while peeking through his fingers at a contestant, too afraid to even see the travesty unfolding before him, I might just lose it. Have these buffoons never heard of clam chowder? Oysters rockefeller? Lobster Mac? Hell, I'm not going to hold it up as a paragon of fine dining, but McDonald's has never been tempted to remove that fluorescent yellow slice of cheese food from their fried fish sandwich. Culinary rules are constantly broken, often with great results, and, like all rules, are there to be tested.

Some of the rules of the kitchen do have bits of wisdom in them, but they should never be blindly accepted, especially if the source can't give you a reason for it. Try it for yourself. I often find that by removing these extra steps I can take loads of work out of a recipe. Probably they're right sometimes, and their result is a little bit better. But, if I can produce a dish that is 98% as good while cutting out 20% of the prep and cleanup, I'll take that every time.

The same goes for mixing ingredients. There are plenty of dos and don'ts, but nobody really knows what they're talking about. If you think two flavors sound good together, mix them. It might be great. And, if it isn't, you'll know better next time. In the end, half of the joy in the kitchen comes from exactly that: cooking by instinct. The more you try, the more you test, the better you get. It's as simple as that.

To that end, you'll find that in this book that I am often not precise with cooking times and other such things that I find to be too variable for me to give you exact measurements. It is purposeful. Between your different stove, the size of your dice, the thickness of your chicken breast, the pan you choose, the quantity of oil, and everything else, I just can't tell you exactly how long or how hot to cook things. And, beyond that, I want you to learn to experience and love the process. If I were to use an infrared thermometer to tell you exactly how hot your pan should be when you put in a zucchini sliced with millimeter precision, I may be able to tell you exactly how it will cook, but you won't learn a damn thing, and you certainly won't have any fun.

None of these recipes are gospel. They're delicious and they work, but your tastes will never be exactly the same as mine, so you should feel free to play with them and make them suit your style of cooking and your style of eating. The best way to learn to love cooking is to trust your instincts and to play in the kitchen. Use these recipes as a guide, not as exacting rules. After all, it's only food, and it'll probably come out great.

COSTA RICAN RECIPES

GALLO PINTO

If you have ever set foot in Costa Rica, it's a safe bet that you've eaten gallo pinto. This dish of simply seasoned rice and beans was served at every Costa Rican breakfast table I ever sat at, and with good reason. Gallo pinto, which translates to spotted rooster, is a great way to start the morning: it is inexpensive, hearty, and a perfect way to use up leftover rice and beans. A quick trip to the skillet with a bit of Salsa Lizano, and those leftovers are transformed into a delicious breakfast. To complete the table, add scrambled eggs, fresh fruit, and good, strong coffee. It is a simple breakfast, and one that I could eat every day.

For those of you that haven't previously had the pleasure, Salsa Lizano is a lightly spiced, slightly sweet, brown sauce made from a variety of vegetables and spices. For me, my experiences in Costa Rican could never be completely divorced from the flavor of salsa Lizano. It is delicious in soups, on eggs, and is what gives Costa Rican gallo pinto its unique savor. You can find it at many hispanic grocers and online.

INGREDIENTS:

2 tablespoons neutral oil
½ red bell pepper, diced
½ small yellow onion, diced
¼ cup cilantro, roughly chopped
2 cups cooked rice
1 cup cooked black beans (or from a can)
1/4 cup Salsa Lizano

DIRECTIONS:

Cook the diced onion and bell pepper over medium-high heat until the onions are translucent and the edges are beginning to brown.

Add the cilantro, reserving a bit to garnish, and cook for a minute more.

Add the rice, beans, and salsa lizano. Stir together well and allow to fry, stirring occasionally for two more minutes.

Remove from heat, salt to taste, and garnish with a bit more chopped cilantro.

Serve with eggs, tortillas, fresh fruit, and strong coffee for a proper Tico breakfast. And definitely put that bottle of salsa lizano on the table, I guarantee you'll want a bit more.

Chifrijos is essentially a Costa Rican taco bowl. Made with crispy, fried pork belly, rice, beans, sofrito, and avocado, it is a dish you will want to eat every day. The name chifrijos is a portmanteau of chicharrones and frijoles, fried pork belly and beans, a delightful name for a delighful snack food created to soak up the booze in the cantinas of San José.

INGREDIENTS:

Pork Belly:
2 lbs. pork belly
1 lime
4 cloves garlic
1 tsp cumin
2 tbsp high-heat oil
Rice:
2 cups rice
2 cups water
1 cup broth
Beans:
2 cans red beans or kidney beans
2 cloves garlic, crushed
1 tsp cumin
2 tsp salsa lizano (optional)
Sofrito:
½ white onion, diced
4 roma tomatoes, seeded and finely diced
2 tbsp cilantro, chopped
Juice of 1 lime
To Serve:
1 large avocado, sliced
2 limes, sliced into wedges
1 bag of tortilla chips

DIRECTIONS:

Pork Belly:
Slice the pork belly into 1-2" cubes and marinate with cumin, garlic, and lime for at least an hour. In a large, deep skillet, over medium-high heat, add the 2 tablespoons of oil and the pork belly. Fry the pork belly until it is nice and crispy. This will take some time and will render a lot of oil. Remove the pieces of pork belly as they finish cooking. Place them on a plate covered in paper towels to allow them to drain some fat. Salt liberally.
Rice:
Cook the rice in a covered saucepan. Place 2 cups rice, 2 cups water, and 1 cup broth on a burner over medium heat. When the water comes to a boil, reduce the heat to low and simmer for 10 minutes. When those 10 minutes are up, turn off the heat and allow the rice to steam, covered, for another 10 minutes.
Beans:
Empty the 2 cans of beans with all the liquid in the can into a skillet and place it over low heat. Add 2 crushed cloves of garlic, 1 teaspoon ground cumin, and 2 teaspoons salsa Lizano. Simmer this, stirring occasionally, until warm and delicious.
Sofrito:
Finely dice the ½ white onion and 4 roma tomatoes and put them in a bowl. Add 2 tbsp finely chopped cilantro and the juice of 1 lime. Sprinkle with salt, mix together, and set aside
Serving:
Construct each serving in a bowl by layering rice, beans, and pork belly. Top with a dollop of sofrito, some avocado slices, a few chips, and additional lime wedges.

SOPA NEGRA

Sopa Negra exemplifies what I love about Costa Rican food: it is a simple dish which does not rely on aggressive spices, instead letting the ingredients subtly speak for themselves. It is a delightful soup made with black beans, lots of vegetables, and a splash of salsa Lizano. It is quite a warming dish, often served in the cooler areas of the country, and is best eaten topped with some fresh cilantro, another splash of salsa lizano, and a boiled egg. Or, if you want to take on an extra challenge, you can poach an egg right in the soup. If you are looking for a simple, clean, and delicious dinner, look no further.

INGREDIENTS:

1 lb. dry black beans
6 cups vegetable broth
1 cup red bell pepper, diced
1 cup white onion, diced
1 cup celery, diced
1 cup carrot, diced
½ cup cilantro, finely chopped
4 cloves garlic, minced

Serve with:
1 boiled egg per serving
Sour cream
Salsa Lizano
Rice
Corn Tortillas

DIRECTIONS:

Put the beans in a container and cover with 2 inches of water. Allow them to soak for around 4 hours. If they take up all the water, add more until they are just covered.

Once soaked, add the beans to a large pot on the stove along with any remaining soaking water. Add 6 cups of vegetable broth and bring to a boil. Reduce the heat and simmer covered until the beans are fully cooked and soft, around 1 hour.

Add the vegetables and herbs to the pot and simmer for an additional 30 minutes, or until the carrots are cooked through.

Serve with a boiled egg, sliced avocado, sour cream, and salsa lizano.

Arroz con pollo was the very first Costa Rican food that I ate. I was young, probably only eight or nine years old, when we first visited. My Aunt had been many times and was good friends with a family that lived in the Alajuela area. The night that our plane landed, they invited us over to their home and served us this simple, delicious dish of chicken cooked with rice, vegetables, and a few spices. It was my first international culinary experience, and I can still remember how amazing and different it was for my young mind.

The name means simply rice with chicken, though it is also sometimes called arroz con siempre (rice with always) due to its regularity in the Costa Rican diet. With how delicious this dish is, it is no wonder that it took that place, as the "always" dish. It might just become that in your kitchen too.

INGREDIENTS:

1 whole chicken, broken down
1 tsp garlic
½ tsp cumin
¼ tsp black pepper
¼ tsp cayenne pepper
2 tsp salt
¼ cup neutral oil

1 green bell pepper
1 red bell pepper
1 medium yellow onion
1 jalapeno
1.5 cups rice
3 cloves garlic
2 cups chicken stock
2 tbsp tomato paste
1 ¼ cups water

DIRECTIONS:

Break down the chicken into 8 pieces and pat dry. Coat the pieces evenly with the spices and brown them in oil in a large, heavy-bottomed pot (around 5 minutes on each side), and remove them to a plate to rest.

Cook the vegetables in the oil for 5 or 6 minutes. Then add the rice and garlic and toast for around 1 minute.

Add the stock, water, and tomato paste and bring the mixture to a boil. Return the chicken to the pot, cover, and reduce the heat to medium-low. Cook like this for 20-25 minutes, until most of the water is absorbed.

Remove from heat and allow to stand for 10 minutes before serving for the rice to finish cooking.

OLLA DE CARNE

Olla de Carne, which translates to pot of beef, is Costa Rican comfort food at its finest. Slow-simmered beef and a wide variety of vegetables (traditionally whatever was abundant at the time) creates a stew which warms you to your core and feels so, so nourishing. Similar to French pot-au-feu, Spanish olla podrida, or really any other beef stew, olla de carne is a dish which traditionally takes a long time to prepare. Tough pieces of meat are added to a pot with lots of vegetables and are allowed to stew until all are tender and floating in a rich and flavorful broth.

Made with beef, potatoes, plantains, sweet potatoes, squash, chicken broth, and sofrito, this stew is delicious unlike anything I've had before. I don't remember where I picked up the tip about using chicken broth, but it creates a uniquely savory flavor. Add to that the plantains and chayote squash, and you have a dish that is miles apart from your standard beef stew. Given that this dish was traditionally made with whatever was available at the time, there are many other common ingredients you can feel free to add, such as taro, cassava, corn, other squashes, or really whatever sounds good.

INGREDIENTS:

1 lb. stew beef
½ large white onion, diced
1 red bell pepper, diced
½ cup tightly packed cilantro, finely chopped
4 cloves garlic, minced
1 lb. sweet potatoes, cut into 1" cubes
1 lb. red potatoes, cut into 1" cubes
1 carrot cut in 1" slices
2 green plantains, cut in 1" slices
2 chayote squash, cut into 1" cubes (optional)
8 cups chicken broth

DIRECTIONS:

Heat a large pot over medium-high heat. Add a splash of oil and the stew beef. Cook until nicely browned and remove the meat from the pot.

Reduce the heat to medium and quickly add the onion, garlic, cilantro, and red bell pepper. Cook these, stirring often, until the onions begin to turn translucent.

Return the meat to the pot and add the potatoes, sweet potatoes, carrots, plantains, and squash, as well as 8 cups of chicken broth.

Simmer the stew for around 30 minutes or until the potatoes are cooked through.

This salad just tastes like nutrition (in a good way). I may have already started sounding like a broken record when it comes to Costa Rican food, but like many other dishes in the cuisine, this salad is uncomplicated and perfect. Made simply with fresh ingredients, it is wholesome and delicious.

This dish is a great side with just about any Costa Rican meal, and is particularly good on a casado plate. You'll have to check out the next recipe for more information about what that means.

INGREDIENTS:

½ head of cabbage
¼ cup olive oil
¼ cup lime juice (2-3 limes)
¼ cup cilantro, packed and minced
½ tsp salt
1 tsp red pepper flakes (optional)
½ cup roma tomatoes, seeded and diced

DIRECTIONS:

Slice the cabbage in half and cut out the stem. Slice one half as thinly as possible and further slice into 3-inch segments.

In a large salad bowl, combine the sliced cabbage, minced cilantro, and tomatoes. Add the olive oil, lime juice, salt, and red pepper flakes.

Toss the salad and allow it to wilt for around 30 minutes before serving.

Casado is not so much a dish as it is a meal. In Costa Rica, lunch is typically the largest meal of the day, and the casado plate is a popular option.

The origins are a bit cloudy, as they often are, but the word translates directly to "married," or "married man." Casado is a mixed plate, typically with rice and beans plus some sort of meat and vegetables or other starches. One idea is that these plates were created to mimic the sort of homemade meals that a married man, with a wife back home to cook for him, might enjoy. Another theory is that these plates are based on the lunches that wives would pack for their husbands, lovingly wrapped in a banana leaf, when they went off to their jobs as laborers. Or it may simply refer to the marrying of a variety of dishes on a single plate. Regardless of the actual origin, what you have is a large plate perfect for dinner or a hearty lunch. Just make sure you have time for a nap afterward.

What I have for you here is actually two recipes for Costa Rican dishes that you can use to fill out a casado plate: a Costa Rican cabbage slaw and a recipe for stewed pork. You'll have to figure out your own recipes for fried plantains, rice, and beans to make the full plate, but I believe in you. Or check out the chifrijos recipe on page 90.

INGREDIENTS:

2 lbs. pork stew meat
½ cup finely chopped cilantro (~1 bunch)
1 red bell pepper, diced
1 medium white onion, diced
5 cloves garlic, minced
Juice of 1 lime
1 tsp oregano
½ tsp black pepper
Salt, to taste

DIRECTIONS:

Heat a large pot over medium-high heat. Add a splash of oil and then toss in the pork stew meat as well as the oregano and black pepper. Sear the pork until browned on all sides.

Add the onion, garlic, bell pepper, cilantro, and lime. Add water to just cover, and simmer, uncovered, until the pork is tender and the water is reduced by half or more, around 45 minutes.

Add salt to taste.

Serve with fried plantains, rice, beans, and cabbage salad for a perfect casado plate.

Tres Leches Cake (pastel de tres leches) is an immensely popular dessert throughout Central and South America. The origin of the cake is a matter of debate, and while it definitely did not originate in Costa Rica (at least I haven't heard anyone argue that), that is where I first ate it, so that's the cuisine I am going to toss it in with. I can't remember the exact occasion that I first ate this amazing cake, but I do know that it was the only thing I wanted on my birthday for years afterward. We baked this cake again for my first birthday in the bus and ate it in the middle of the Mojave desert. It was every bit as wonderful as I remembered.

INGREDIENTS:

Cake:
1 cup flour
1 ½ tsp baking powder
¼ tsp salt
5 eggs, separated
1 cup sugar
1 tsp vanilla
⅓ cup milk

Syrup:
1 cup condensed milk
1 cup evaporated milk
1 cup heavy cream

Frosting:
1 cup heavy cream
1 tsp sugar
¼ tsp vanilla

Garnish:
Ground Cinnamon or
Sliced Strawberries

DIRECTIONS:

First, you need to bake the cake. In a large mixing bowl, stir together 1 cup flour, 1 ½ tsp baking powder, and ¼ tsp salt.

In another mixing bowl, beat the egg yolks (with an electric mixer) with ¾ cup sugar until they turn pale yellow. Add ⅓ cup milk and 1 tsp vanilla and mix well.

Rinse the mixer well to remove any yolk. In yet another mixing bowl beat the egg whites with ¼ cup sugar until they form stiff peaks.

Mix the egg yolks and flour mixture until well combined. Gently fold in the egg whites with a spatula until only just combined. Pour the batter into the lightly greased cake pans and get ready to bake. Typically, tres leches is baked in a large pan like a casserole dish, but we use two smaller cake pans, 8" and 8" and a 6".

Bake for around 35-40 minutes at 350 degrees, or until a toothpick poked into the center comes out clean.

Allow the cakes to cool, and then poke holes all over the top with a fork. Mix the tres leches together to make your syrup, and pour it over the top. Put the cake in the refrigerator and allow it to soak for at least a couple hours and as much as a couple days.

When you are ready to serve, beat the heavy cream, sugar, and vanilla until it holds nice peaks. Either make a nice layer of whipped cream on top of your cake in the pan, or remove the cake from the pan and frost it on the top and sides. Dust the cake with ground cinnamon or garnish with sliced strawberries.

FORGET FAMILY RECIPES

CREPES

Crepes were my father's Sunday morning specialty. He would crank them out by the dozen, while all of us kids sat at the table, scarfing them down and battling each other to get the next one fresh out of the pan, stuffing ourselves until our stomachs hurt. He served in the same style he had them growing up, with a good swipe of butter and lots of freshly grated maple sugar. Crepes are also Ayana's favorite breakfast, but she takes a more continental approach, and prefers lemon juice and sugar. As an adult, I still get a stomach ache when I eat sweets for breakfast, so I like a savory filling, like ham and cheese. No matter how you eat them, they are simple to throw together with what's already in your pantry, and they are always, always delicious. This recipes makes enough to give two people a stomach ache.

INGREDIENTS:

1 cup flour
2 eggs
1½ cups milk
2 tbsp neutral oil or melted butter
Pinch of salt
¼ tsp vanilla, optional

DIRECTIONS:

Add your dry ingredients to a large mixing bowl, and stir them together. Add the eggs, and beat them well. Pour over the milk, and mix until the batter is smooth.

Heat a 10-12" non-stick pan to medium-low. Grease with butter or, for simplicity's sake, cooking spray. I like to use around ¼ cup batter per crepe, but this makes relatively small crepes (use more if you would like them larger). Pour the batter into the center of the greased pan and swirl it to spread the batter into a large, thin circle.

When the edges of the crepe are cooked, but not crispy (around 60 seconds), flip it over. Cook the other side for 20-30 seconds, and remove to a plate. Re-grease the pan, pour the next scoop of batter in, and, while that is cooking, finish the crepe that just came out.

For the Forget family classic, give the still-warm crepe a good swab with a pat of butter and then sprinkle heavily with maple sugar. For something a bit more French, replace the maple sugar with white sugar and lemon juice. Or fill it with cheese and sausage, or fresh fruit and whipped cream—whatever your heart desires.

FORGET FAMILY ARTICHOKE SAUCE

Artichokes are Ayana's favorite food. Fortunately, when it came to courting her, my family had already stacked the deck in my favor by providing me with the recipe for the best MFin' artichoke dipping sauce out there. Seriously, once you taste this, you will literally throw your garlic butter in the garbage (okay, figuratively).

While it may not seem like much at first glance, wait until you try it before passing judgment. Something magical happens when you combine these simple ingredients. Just make sure you have enough artichokes, as you aren't going to want to stop eating it.

INGREDIENTS:

½ cup mayonnaise
½ tsp garlic powder
½ tsp Italian herb mix
2 tsp white wine vinegar
Salt + Pepper to taste

DIRECTIONS:

Mix this up and toss it in the fridge at least an hour before dinner to allow the flavors to meld.

Serve it with warm, steamed artichokes. That's it. Enjoy.

GREEN CHILE, SHRIMP, AND CORN CHOWDER

There is not a whole lot to say about this recipe, except that it is exquisite. It wasn't passed down from my great grandfather or anything, I just threw it together one cold, autumn night because it sounded kind of good, and it totally knocked our socks off. While its history in the family may not be long right now, it will be when my grandkids are still making it.

This is a chowder for the Southwest: a delicious broth infused with the flavors of green chile, corn, and shrimp, all carried with a hearty backbone of potatoes, onions, and cream. Let New England have their clam chowder, I'll take this.

INGREDIENTS:

1 lb. shrimp
1 cup fresh or frozen sweet corn
1 medium yellow onion, diced
4 cloves of garlic, minced
2 medium russet potatoes, cut into ½" cubes
1¼ cup roasted green chiles
½ tsp cumin
½ tsp oregano
3 tbsp butter
2 tbsp flour
1 qt light stock (fish, shrimp, vegetable, etc.)
2 cups half & half
1 tbsp white wine vinegar

DIRECTIONS:

Cook the potatoes, onion, and garlic in 3 tbsp of butter in a large, heavy-bottomed pot over medium heat until the onion begins to become translucent. Then add the flour to the pot and stir, allowing it to cover everything. Cook, stirring occasionally, for a few minutes until the flour begins to brown.

Add the stock to the pot, followed by the green chiles, corn, cumin, oregano, and half & half. Bring to a gentle boil and then reduce the heat to low and simmer for 10 minutes.

Add the shrimp and allow them to cook through, around 10 minutes more. Turn off heat, add the vinegar, and adjust seasoning with salt and pepper to taste.

Serve with crusty bread or crackers.

Perhaps the meal that I most associate with my childhood is caesar salad and buttered noodles. My father developed this quick and easy dressing recipe, and we probably ate it two or three times a week. It was cheap, easy to make on a busy weeknight, it fed the whole clan, and it was damn delicious. Once you have these ingredients, it is really easy to throw together an awesome salad. And, if you want to turn a simple caesar salad into a show-stopping side, try grilling it.

INGREDIENTS:

Dressing:
¼ cup mayonnaise
1 tsp dijon mustard
1 tbsp olive oil
1 tbsp fresh lemon juice
½ tsp anchovy paste (do not skip this)
1 large clove of garlic, minced
½ tsp freshly ground black pepper
½ cup parmesan, grated
1 large head of romaine lettuce
Croutons, preferrably homemade and pan-fried

DIRECTIONS:

Dressing: In a bowl, mix the mayonnaise, dijon, minced garlic, olive oil, lemon juice, anchovy paste, and black pepper. Allow this to sit a while for the flavors to come together.

For a standard salad, rinse the romaine and chop it into nice, bite-sized pieces. Set the lettuce on top of the dressing, and then toss to coat. Grate the parmesan over the top as well as some additional black pepper, add the croutons and any protein you might like, and serve.

To grill, just split a head of romaine, rub it with a little olive oil, and slap it on the grill until you have some good char. Then drizzle it with dressing and sprinkle over some parmesan cheese and freshly grated black pepper. Delicious.

THE FAMILY TATERS

These are the mashed potatoes that were served at all family gatherings when I was growing up, and I'm pretty sure they are the best out there. I know that I have a certain amount of bias, seeing as these are the taters of my youth, but I can assure you that every person I've ever served them to has said to me something to the effect of, "damn, those are some good potatoes." This recipe is what I make for big events, so it'll likely need to be scaled for your weeknight dinner. That said, if you make the full five pounds, you'll eat the full five pounds, and the only thing that will be upset is potentially your waistline.

INGREDIENTS:

5 lbs. red potatoes
2 tbsp garlic, minced
8 tbsp butter
1 cup grated parmesan cheese
2½ cups sour cream
Salt + Pepper to taste

DIRECTIONS:

Cut the potatoes into around 2-inch cubes and add to a large pot of boiling, well-salted water. Boil until fork tender, remove from heat, and drain the water from the pot.

Return the potatoes to the pot and add 1 stick of butter cut into 4 pieces. Mix this around as it melts. Add the 1 cup of grated parmesan cheese (use the good stuff), and mix well, so that this can melt and release its oils. Add the garlic and sour cream and stir well to combine. This is a good time for the first round of salt and pepper. Add about as much as you think you will want (you will probably double or triple it before the end).

By now, your potatoes will likely be about half mashed, but you can bring out the potato masher to finish the job. Mash the potatoes to your preferred consistency. For me, with waxy potatoes, I prefer a rustic mash that still has some nice chunks in it.

When your potatoes are as mashed as you like them, taste for salt and pepper levels. I usually end up doing at least two, maybe three or four rounds of small additions before I hit my ideal level.

MOM'S LEMON CHICKEN

For me, this recipe is my childhood. Growing up this dish was, at least in my mind, Mom's specialty. It was one of those dinners that we didn't have every week, but every time we did eat it, I wondered why we didn't have it every night. Lightly breaded chicken pieces are cooked with lemon, onions, and thyme, and then served over egg noodles and topped with the delicious pan gravy. It isn't complicated, it isn't hard, but it is hard to beat.

INGREDIENTS:

3 tbsp flour
½ tsp salt
¼ tsp pepper
¼ tsp garlic powder
2 lbs. chicken tenderloins or breast cutlets
2 tbsp olive oil
1 medium yellow onion, quartered and sliced
1 tablespoon butter
1 cup chicken broth
3 tbsp fresh lemon juice
½ tsp thyme
lemon wedges
2 tbsp parsley, finely chopped

DIRECTIONS:

Mix the flour, garlic powder, salt, and pepper on a plate, and dredge the chicken in it. Reserve the excess seasoned flour.

Bring a large skillet to medium heat. When hot, add the olive oil and then the chicken. Brown the chicken on both sides, around 4 minutes each, and then remove it to a plate.

Add the butter to the skillet and then the sliced onion. Cook, stirring occasionally, until the onion is softened and slightly translucent, 2-3 minutes. Then add the remaining flour to the pan with the onions and cook for around 1 minute. Next add the broth, 2 tablespoons of fresh lemon juice, and the thyme. Stir this together until it makes a nice gravy.

Return the chicken to the pan, as well as any juices, reduce heat to medium-low, cover, and simmer around 5 minutes until the chicken is cooked through.

Remove from heat and plate the chicken. Add the remaining 1 tablespoon of lemon juice and the chopped parsley to the sauce in the pan, stir together, and adjust seasoning. Serve the chicken over egg noodles with a scoop of the gravy from the pan.

DAD'S STEAK BEARNAISE

What on earth is more luxurious than a fine piece of grilled beef drizzled with a hot butter sauce? Flavored with tarragon, shallots, and white wine vinegar, bearnaise sauce adds both creamy decadence and a pleasant acidity to cut through the fat of the beef. I first tasted this dish at my father's 60th birthday. We all went to a steakhouse and ordered as he did: filet bearnaise. To this day I don't know if there is anything I'd rather eat. That particular event was extraordinary, but the practice, my father leading us boys to good food, was one that happened often all through our lives. He taught us all from a young age to appreciate a good meal and to always taste new dishes, even if we thought we wouldn't like them. As a result, all four of us boys grew up comfortable and happy in the kitchen, and I was sent down this long, winding path of culinary exploration.

INGREDIENTS:

½ lb. salted butter, melted
½ cup white wine vinegar
½ cup sherry
2 large shallots
4 tbsp tarragon
10 peppercorns
3 egg yolks
1 whole egg

DIRECTIONS:

Boil the vinegar, sherry, shallots, peppercorns, and 3 tbsp tarragon until the liquid is reduced to around ½ cup. Strain and discard the solids.

Allow to cool and then whisk the beaten eggs into the vinegar. You can temper the eggs first by stirring in a bit of the hot vinegar. Then put the mixture over a double boiler and continue to whisk.

When it just begins to thicken, slowly whisk in the butter over 4-5 additions. When a beautiful, thick consistency is reached, remove from heat.

Finish with the remaining 1 tbsp tarragon (finely chopped). You can also add additional salt and/or white wine vinegar if the taste isn't quite right. I would suggest tasting, and if the taste is too buttery, add 1 tsp white wine vinegar. If you used salted butter, the salt level should be fine.

This recipe makes enough for many steaks, but it is also great on fish, vegetables, eggs—really just about anything. Leftovers can be gently reheated in a pan or even the microwave

This here is Grandma's Impossible Pie. We used to eat it every year at Christmas, and I have recently learned why: the "impossible" part of the name refers to how it must be impossible for such an easy pie to be so dang good, which makes it the perfect second dessert to feed a big family. Christmas and Thanksgiving feasts are a lot of work, why not let at least one dish be easy?

Seriously though, all you have to do to make this amazing pie is throw these ingredients together and toss it in the oven. No crust, no complicated recipe, just a couple minutes of prep and half an hour of baking. You really can't argue with that.

INGREDIENTS:

4 eggs
½ cup flour
½ tsp baking powder
pinch salt
4 tbsp butter
1½ cups sugar
2 cups milk
1 cup dried, shredded coconut (unsweetened)

DIRECTIONS:

Mix all ingredients except the milk and coconut in a large mixing bowl. Beat well, then add the milk and coconut, and beat again.

Pour the mixture into a 9-inch pie pan and bake at 350 degrees for 30-35 minutes. That's it.

A DAY IN THE BUSLIFE

Buslife is a highly glamorized way of living. These days the internet is overflowing with pictures of beautiful young people living out of their vehicles amidst gorgeous natural landscapes. Back when I was on the outside I always wondered what an actual day was like for them. Not the photoshoot day at the hot spring where the camera is positioned perfectly to create an illusion of solitude, not the day that they're shooting drone video of the bus cruising through the desert, kicking up a plume of red dust, but a regular damn day. What does a Tuesday in November look like, when it's raining outside and you aren't at some gorgeous national park? While I don't have the space here to tell you about every kind of buslife day, I'll do my best to give a little bit of insight about what it's really like.

In a lot of ways, buslife actually is that magical fantasy that you see on social media, with the amazing campsites in beautiful places. Believe it or not, those internet dreams are actually based in reality. During our time in the bus (about a year and a half at the time of writing), we've had the opportunity to park in some truly magnificent places, be it feet from the ocean, the center of a windswept lakebed, or beside an alpine lake. But that certainly isn't always the case. Sometimes it is truly magical, but generally buslife is a whole lot like regular life, and often quite a bit less glamorous. There is freedom to choose your own schedule, the opportunity to adventure wherever you want, and truly endless beauty, but there is also plenty of anxiety and extra work, and a whole lot of stinky stuff.

A typical morning starts for us blissfully absent an alarm. We wake up generally not too long after the sun, and after a few stretches and yawns, one of us will get out of bed to make a pot of coffee. If the weather is nice and we are someplace pretty, we might drink our coffee outside in our camp chairs. As you can imagine, this is pretty wonderful when we're parked at a lakeside campsite in the summer, and a whole lot less desirable when we wake up on a drizzly January morning in the Cracker Barrel parking lot.

After coffee (and sometimes before), we generally get to work. For me that means opening up a notebook or my laptop and setting to the myriad tasks of writing, editing photos, maintaining our websites, managing social media, or any of the other thousands of tasks required to write a cookbook and manage a business. Ayana's work has been more varied through our time in the bus so

far, and has included making jewelry, practicing natural dreamwork, life coaching, and caring for children, as well as staying on top of her social media channels and doing a much better job than me of maintaining real relationships with her friends and family.

Most days that work goes until about sunset. Given that we have the luxury of making our own schedules, we do take breaks for things like eating lunch together, exercise, phone calls, walks, or whatever we feel like we need that day, but most of it is spent working. It has been an important realization for me, as someone who has always struggled to put enough creative words on the page, that these breaks are very important to my productivity, and that rest is an integral part of work.

For years, I burned myself out trying to be productive with every second of my day. It was largely simple decisions, like instead of watching a fun show to relax, I would choose a documentary related to a project I was working on so that I might learn something useful while I watched.

Little choices like that don't seem significant by themselves, but when you never totally clock out, you smother your inner creative. The greatest boon of buslife for me has been recognizing that on those days when I really don't feel like I have anything to say or any energy to build something, the best solution for my mental health and my productivity is to fuck off and play video games all afternoon. That wasted time, when I can truly turn off my work brain and accept that I am doing nothing of value, always leads to a creative breakthrough shortly thereafter. Living in the bus and not being on anyone else's schedule let me explore that, and I am very grateful for it. So, most afternoons of buslife are spent working, but some are spent exploring or exercising, and others are spent doing that thing that we all need more of and few of us make time for anymore: really relaxing.

As the sun dips toward the horizon, we typically clock out and pour ourselves a cocktail. On a perfect day in the bus, we would be camped with some friends and might climb up to the deck for a rooftop happy hour. The greatest gift of traveling, no matter where you are, is sharing a drink or a meal with new friends, often someplace truly beautiful, and buslife gives us plenty of those opportunities. A sunset cocktail and some conversation on the rooftop is about as good as it gets, and we do our best to take advantage of every such moment.

Eventually the sun goes down, it gets a bit chilly, and the bellies start to rumble, which means it's time for me to go back to work. I do the majority of my recipe work in the evenings, saving the days for writing and assorted business work. Nearly every night I am working on something. Sometimes it's a brand new recipe, that I am just starting to experiment with, and sometimes it's a dish that I am already proficient with, and my focus is instead on fine-tuning, plating, and photographing it, but I rarely cook just for fun these days. Fortunately, this sort of work feels a whole lot more like play to me than anything else I've ever done, and it takes a lot longer to burn me out. There are definitely nights where we eat macaroni and cheese or quesadillas because I have just had it with cooking for a while, but those are relatively few and far between. Either way, dinner is always made and always enjoyed. If we're lucky, the meal I'm working on is something really tasty, and if we're doubly fortunate we have some friends around to share it with.

After dinner, our buslife is about the same as it was before. We might play a board game or have another drink and some conversation if we're with friends, or we might just read or watch TV and go to sleep.

Life in the bus follows similar rhythms to our old lives, the main difference being that we simply have more freedom and more choice. We don't have to go to work each morning as soon as we wake up, but we do need to work each day if we want to keep on living well. We are free to go nearly anywhere we want, but those moves mean packing up, resupplying, and travel time, which usually takes a whole day, so we don't typically move but once a week. And, in spite of all of this freedom and the lack of a structured schedule being forced on us, we still go through the same emotional cycles. We both still have days that are inexplicably bad. I'm prone to grouchiness, and living on the road certainly hasn't made that disappear. Before, when we were working all the time for someone else, it was easy to blame our jobs when we came home in a crummy mood, but now it seems those feelings may have been misplaced. Even as the decider of my own destiny, I still have bad days in which I am inexplicably irritable after work. It seems that these things just happen, to all of us, all of the time.

Additionally, there is a huge amount of discipline required to keep a good schedule when you have full control of your days. If you aren't careful, it is pretty easy to fall into a pattern of relaxing a little bit too much, which inevitably leads to listlessness, and often depression. From a young age we are all trained to primarily live our lives in service to external goals. It is not an easy transition to start setting those goals for yourself, and in many ways it is much more difficult. I wouldn't have it any other way, but I had years of practice during the empty winter months between fire

seasons, when the only thing holding back seasonal depression was travel and a strict regimen of activities that really mattered to me.

In the end, this life pretty quickly became regular for us. Like our old lives, there is always work to do, there are always chores, there is always concern about money, and there is always that most pernicious of human experiences: boredom. As much as we travel, adventure, and chase our dreams, we are still always seeking that next step, the next piece that will finally finish the puzzle and make us happy forever—until we get close to it and spot another, shinier piece just a little further along. It is easy, if you are not vigilant, to lose sight of the beauty around you, even when it is as immense as that which we experience on the road.

Buslife is truly magical, and I am so thankful that I get to live it every day, and to share it with my love. But, just like every other way of living, the joys of life on the road can be quickly lost in a haze of work, money woes, and general ennui. What matters most, no matter how you're living, is taking the time to slow down, take a breath, and enjoy the now, whether that means taking the night to play a board game or watch a movie with new friends, or just having a cocktail and enjoying the sunset before dinner. Those were some of the things we loved most before we moved into the bus, and the only thing that's really changed is that now we get to do them in a new place each week. Lasting happiness is never really found at the end of that path where you expect it. In my experience, it only comes from inside, from taking time to appreciate what is good in your life here and now. It's an old idea perhaps, that real happiness is only born from practicing gratitude, but it's one that I remind myself of often.

VIETNAMESE RECIPES

In its simplest form, cháo is a soup made with broth, rice, and maybe a few pieces of ginger and scallion. As it simmers, the starches released from the rice thicken the soup, and the individual rice grains soften and bloom. A good broth or stock is important, as that is the primary flavoring agent of the soup, but the delicate flavors of scallion and ginger accent a simple store-bought broth nicely. I also like to add a serrano pepper for additional complexity and a little bit of heat, but that part is non-traditional, and definitely optional. If you want to make a meal of it, adding a few chicken thighs and an onion makes this soup hearty enough to be a standalone dinner.

INGREDIENTS:

¾ cup long-grain rice
2 ½ quarts vegetable or chicken stock
6 quarter-sized slices of ginger
4 scallions, white part only, sliced coarsely
1 serrano pepper, sliced coarsely (optional)

With Chicken:
1 lb. chicken thighs, chopped into large cubes
1½ tbsp fish sauce
1 tbsp neutral oil
1 yellow onion, quartered and sliced thin
2 tbsp cilantro, chopped finely
2 scallions, greens only , chopped finely

DIRECTIONS:

Put the rice in a large pot and cover with 1" water. Stir the rice a few times, and drain the water. Repeat this process, but do not stir the rice the second time around.

Add stock, ginger, serrano, and scallions to the pot, cover, and bring to a boil. Uncover the pot, reduce heat to medium-high, and allow to boil gently for around 5 minutes.

Reduce the heat to medium-low, for a gentle simmer, cover, and cook for 1 hour.

After the hour is done, the broth should be nicely thickened by the starch from the rice. It will thicken more as it cools. Remove and discard the ginger, scallions, and serrano. Add salt to taste.

With Chicken:
Marinate the chicken in the fish sauce for 15 minutes.

Cook the onion with the oil in a skillet over medium heat for a few minutes until nicely fragrant and lightly browned at the edges. Add the chicken and cook until browned on the outside and cooked through.

Add all contents of the pan to the finished rice soup, including any juices.

Variously known as spring rolls, salad rolls, and summer rolls, you are likely familiar with this delicious appetizer. Shrimp, vermicelli noodles, and fresh herbs are bundled up in a rice paper and dipped in that perfect dipping sauce, nước chấm. It is hard to beat, particularly in warm climates.

INGREDIENTS:

~24 medium shrimp, peeled and cooked
½ lb. fine rice noodles, cooked and cooled
Cilantro
Mint
Basil
Chives
2 cucumbers
Rice papers (1 packet)

Nước Chấm:
2 tbsp fish sauce
3 tbsp water
1 thai or serrano chili, sliced thin

Lime-Ginger Sauce:
1" ginger, minced
Juice from 1½ limes
2½ tbsp fish sauce
2 tbsp water
1 tbsp sugar

DIRECTIONS:

Making salad rolls is mostly a matter of preparing your mise en place. Having a few extra hands on deck to help with rolling doesn't hurt either. The shrimp are the only cooked ingredient in this, so the directions are mostly about slicing.

The shrimp should be peeled, poached and cooled, then sliced in half lengthwise. You want the nice curled shrimp shape, just a bit thinner.

The cucumber should be peeled, cut into 4" long segments (or as long as your rolls) and then sliced lengthwise into ¼" thick steaks.

The rice noodles should be cooked and cooled—these provide a lot of the filling. The herbs can be used whole, just wash them and have plenty ready.

To make the rolls, you will want a plate with a bit of water next to your work surface. Begin by submerging a rice paper in the plate of water briefly. Remove the rice paper to your work space and allow it to sit and hydrate until it becomes slightly tacky. Then it is ready to work with. Fill the spring roll with a row of shrimp. On top of the shrimp place a cucumber steak, then your herbs, then rice noodles.

Now you are ready to roll it up. Start with the sides. Fold these in. The tacky rice paper will stick to itself and give you more control. Now grab the closer end, fold it over the fillings (not too tightly) and then roll the whole thing up. If your spring rolls are too long, cut them in half to serve.

Dipping Sauces:
For the nước chấm, combine the fish sauce and water, drop in the thinly sliced serrano or thai chili, and allow to sit for 15 minutes to meld the flavors.
For the lime-ginger sauce, combine all the ingredients, dissolve the sugar, and let it sit and meld for about 30 minutes before serving.

Unlike western pancakes, which are made with batter, scallion pancakes are instead made with an unleavened wheat dough, folded through with scallions and fried to a crisp in a skillet. Dipped in a sauce of soy, vinegar, and chili oil, they make an excellent appetizer.

These delicious snacks are enjoyed throughout much of Asia, and the origin is somewhat debated, but probably doesn't matter much in the end. I've stuck them in my Vietnamese section, which isn't wrong, but they could equally be considered among Chinese, Korean, Taiwanese, and other cuisines. Regardless of where they originated, everyone who eats them wants to start making them and selling them back home—probably a good indicator that you ought to give them a shot as well.

INGREDIENTS:

2½ cups flour
1 tbsp sesame oil
1 tsp salt
1 cup hot water
¾ cup scallions, sliced thin (around 2 bunches)
Neutral oil

Dipping sauce:
1 tbsp water
1 tbsp rice vinegar
1 tbsp soy sauce
1 tsp chili oil
½ tsp sugar
¼ tsp crushed red pepper

DIRECTIONS:

Add flour, salt, sesame oil, and water to a mixing and stir to combine. Knead briefly to form a uniform ball of dough, cover, and rest for 1 hour.

Roll the dough flat, lightly brush with oil, and add the scallions. Roll the dough into a cylinder by curling in one edge and rolling it over itself. Coil the cylinder like a cinnamon roll and allow it to rest another 15 minutes.

Work the coiled dough into a ball and slice it into eighths. Ball the eighths individually and roll them very thin.

Bring a skillet to medium heat, add a small amount of oil, and one of the pancakes. Cook until crispy and brown (around 4 minutes), then flip and repeat. Do this with one pancake at a time.

Pancakes can be served whole or sliced into smaller pieces.

Dipping Sauce:
Simply combine ingredients in a small bowl and stir to dissolve sugar.

Bánh xèo (pronounced something like bon say-oh) is a fried Vietnamese rice flour crepe. The name is actually something of an onomatopoeia, as xèo sounds like the batter sizzling in the pan. A simple batter of rice flour, coconut milk, and turmeric is quickly fried and filled with shrimp, bean sprouts, scallions, and other tasty goodies. Then "dragged through the garden" in the local parlance, meaning wrapped in lettuce and fresh herbs, and eaten with the ever-present dipping sauce, nước chấm.

INGREDIENTS:

Batter:
2 cups rice flour
1 tsp salt
½ tsp turmeric
14 oz. coconut milk (1 can)
1 ¼ cups water

Filling:
1½ pounds shrimp, peeled and cooked
½ yellow onion, quartered and sliced
2 cups bean sprouts
1 bunch scallions, sliced thin

Accoutrements:
Basil, Mint, and Cilantro
1 head of green leaf lettuce

Nước Chấm:
2 tbsp fish sauce
3 tbsp water
1 thai or serrano chili, sliced thinly

DIRECTIONS:

Make the batter a few hours before using it. This allows it to hydrate nicely. Simply mix the batter ingredients, cover, and allow to rest.

To make the crepes, heat a skillet over high heat. Add a small amount of oil and pour in roughly ⅓ cup of the batter. If necessary, swirl the pan to allow the batter to spread out nice and thin. Toss the shrimp and onions in immediately.

The crepe is done when cooked through in the center. The edges should be crispy and, when folded, there should be good browned parts of the crepe. Before folding, add some bean sprouts and scallions.

Serve while still hot. To eat, tear off a piece of the crepe, add some fresh herbs from the plate, wrap it up in a piece of lettuce, and either dip in the nước chấm or drizzle some over the top.

Dipping Sauce:
For the nước chấm, combine the fish sauce and water, drop in the thinly sliced serrano or thai chili, and allow to sit for 15 minutes to meld the flavors.

COLD NOODLE BOWL

This is the first Vietnamese dish I ever tried, and to this day remains one one of my favorites: a bowl of cold rice noodles with a salad of lettuce and fresh herbs on the bottom, chicken and thinly sliced vegetables on top, and a bit of dressing. It is hard to beat. And it turns out they're also pretty easy to make at home. There is definitely some prep to get the ingredients in order, but if you just bite the bullet and do the work one night, you can throw these together all week. Which also makes them great for camping trips.

INGREDIENTS:

Chicken:
1½ lbs. Chicken thighs
2 cloves garlic, chopped
3 tbsp fish sauce
¼ cup water

Dressing:
2 tbsp fish sauce
½ cup water
2 tbsp sugar
1 clove garlic, minced
2 tbsp lime juice
1 thai or serrano chili

Bowls:
1 lb. vermicelli rice noodles
1 cucumber, julienned
1 carrot, julienned
2 cups bean sprouts
4 scallions, greens only
1 cup basil, chopped
½ cup mint, chopped
½ cup cilantro, chopped
4-6 large lettuce leaves, chopped small

DIRECTIONS:

Chicken: Marinate the chicken thighs in the garlic, fish sauce, and water for at least 2 hours. Once marinated, grill them or cook them over high heat for a few minutes on each side to brown the outside and cook through. Once cooked, allow them to rest before slicing into serving pieces.

Dressing: make at least half an hour ahead of time to allow the flavors to properly meld. Mix all ingredients and stir until the sugar dissolves. Cover and keep in the refrigerator until serving time.

Noodles: If you have not cooked vermicelli noodles before, they cook extremely quickly. Heat water and drop the noodles in for a minute or two until they are tender, then drain and allow to cool. These can also be done well ahead of time.

To assemble the bowls, start by placing a layer of lettuce and herbs at the bottom of a large bowl. This recipe can make anywhere from 4-8 bowls depending on how large you want them, so divide the ingredients accordingly.

On top of the lettuce and herbs, place a large serving of vermicelli noodles—this will make up the bulk of the dish. Next, artfully arrange the bean sprouts, carrots, cucumber, and chicken on top of the noodles. Sprinkle with chives and dress lightly, but ensure that you keep some of the dressing so that individuals can add more to their bowls more if they would like.

Vietnamese Burnt Caramel Sauce

While not technically burnt, per se, this sauce walks the finest of lines on the edge of burnt. It is a deep, dark, and bittersweet sauce which is responsible for the unforgettably delicious claypot dishes of Vietnam. The caramel is cooked until it turns the color of dark tea or red wine and then quickly cooled by plunging into a dish of water to arrest the cooking at a precise point. Just a spoonful of that bittersweet sauce adds an amazing and unique depth to any protein, as you will see in the following two recipes If you have never made caramel before, know that you need to watch it like a hawk while it is cooking. It will seem for ages like nothing is happening, but the second you take your eyes off it, it will burn. This caramel sauce is particularly fiddly, as it is perfect when it is just toeing the line of burnt. But the depth of flavor achieved by the sweet and bitter nature of a not-quite-burned caramel is absolutely worth the effort.

INGREDIENTS:

2 tbsp water
½ cup sugar
1 tsp rice vinegar

DIRECTIONS:

Begin filling a pot in the sink with cool water. Make sure that the saucepan you will be cooking the caramel sauce in fits inside the pot in the sink.

Heat the 2 tbsp water, ½ cup sugar, and 1 tsp rice vinegar over medium heat, stirring until the sugar dissolves. Stir often for around 5 minutes as the color changes. When it reaches the color of light tea, reduce the heat to medium-low to slow the cooking process. When cooking caramel, things happen by the second, so don't take your eyes off it.

Continue cooking the caramel over medium-low and stirring often. It will continue to darken, and the darkening process will continue to accelerate. The color you are looking for is something between red wine and black coffee. When you hit the red wine appearance, remove the pot from heat and put the bottom into the cool water in the sink. This will immediately arrest the cooking process and stop before you burn it.

Add ¼ cup of water to the caramel and return it to the stove over medium-low heat. The sugar will seize with the addition of water, but as it warms, it will dissolve into the water and give you a nice, dark caramel sauce, thin enough to be spooned or poured. Once it is all dissolved, pour it into a heat-safe container and store it in the fridge until needed. It should taste both sweet and bitter, a bit like good, dark molasses.

CLAYPOT CATFISH

I discovered claypot eel at maybe my second dinner in Vietnam and proceeded to eat it just about every day for the rest of the trip. At the time, I didn't know much about what I was actually ordering, just that each one of those little pots full of eel in a rich, brown sauce was as good as the last. I suggest using catfish for this dish, as it is the most commonly used protein, and is a bit easier to come by than eel, but shrimp, pork, or really anything you put in that pot will come out delicious.

INGREDIENTS:

1 lb. catfish fillets
2 cloves garlic, minced
2 tbsp fish sauce
3 tbsp caramel sauce
(See recipe on p. 117)
1 tsp black pepper
½ yellow onion, quartered and sliced
4 scallions, sliced thin
1 serrano or thai chile, sliced thin
1 tbsp fresh lime juice
¼ cup water

Garnish:
3 scallions, green part only, sliced thin
Lime wedges

DIRECTIONS:

Caramel Sauce:
See recipe on p. 117

Toss everything except the garnish (catfish, fish sauce, onions, scallions, chile, garlic, black pepper, lime juice, water, and caramel sauce) into a large pot over medium heat. Cook covered until the catfish is cooked through, around 8 minutes. Flip the catfish once in the middle. Uncover for the last few minutes to allow the sauce to reduce and thicken.

If the sauce evaporates too quickly, add a bit more water. If it doesn't reduce enough, cook a bit longer uncovered. The sauce should be thick enough to coat the fish and rice well.

Serve with white rice, garnished with scallions and lime wedges.

VIETNAMESE PESTO PASTA WITH CLAYPOT PORK

The flavors in this dish are what I imagine when I think about Vietnamese food: fresh herbs, bittersweet caramel, and pungent fish sauce. It is a complex and multilayered dish, a western-styled pasta dish incorporating the amazing flavors of Vietnam. There are a few steps, but trust me, it's worth it.

INGREDIENTS:

Pesto:
2 cups basil, loosely packed
½ cup mint, loosely packed
½ cup cilantro, loosely packed
¾ cup neutral oil
½ cup scallions, whites only
3 tsp fish sauce
2 clove garlic
2 tbsp fresh lime juice
½ tsp sugar
2 jalapenos, seeded
½ tsp black pepper

Pork Topping:
1 lb. ground pork
1 tbsp chili garlic paste
2 tbsp fish sauce
1 tbsp fresh lime juice
3 tbsp caramel sauce (see recipe on p.117)
½ tsp black pepper
¼ tsp garlic powder

Noodles:
20 oz. dry Udon Noodles

DIRECTIONS:

Caramel Sauce:
See Recipe on p. 117

Pesto:
This pesto is made just like any other. Add all of the ingredients to a food processor and blend it until smooth. Taste, and adjust seasoning as necessary. Some may prefer more fish sauce or more salt.

Ground Pork Topping:
Add the ground pork to a skillet over medium heat. Add all other ingredients and simmer until the pork is cooked through and the sauce is reduced to a thick consistency.

Noodles:
Boil the udon noodles in plenty of well-salted water for around 10 minutes, or until tender. Be aware Udon noodles may cook faster than what you are used to.

Final Dish:
Add the pesto to the drained noodles and stir to coat evenly. Divide the sauced noodles between plates. Top with a scoop of the claypot pork. Garnish with chopped fresh herbs and black pepper. Additional salt, lime, or fish sauce should be available to adjust seasonings to taste.

BANANA TAPIOCA PUDDING

Chè Chuối is a delicious pudding made with coconut milk, tapioca pearls, and ripe bananas. With only 2 tablespoons of added sugar, it is also a rather healthy dessert. Vegan food is not something that we seek out all the time, but I do still celebrate it when I stumble upon or can create an "accidentally vegan" recipe. Because who doesn't love a creamy, delicious pudding that also happens to be vegan and low sugar? That's a serious win in my book.

INGREDIENTS:

½ cup small tapioca pearls
14 oz. coconut milk (1 can)
1 cup water
3 ripe bananas, sliced
2 tbsp sugar (or more, to taste)
1 tbsp sesame seeds, toasted
1 mango, sliced thin

DIRECTIONS:

Soak the tapioca in 3 cups of water for 1 hour. Drain.

Bring 1 cup of water and the tapioca pearls to a boil in a large pot. Reduce to low and allow to simmer a few minutes until translucent.

Add the coconut milk and sugar and cook for 5 minutes, stirring occasionally. Add the sliced bananas, reserving around one half of a banana to garnish. Cook for 5 additional minutes to allow the banana to soften and flavor the pudding. Taste, and add more sugar if desired.

Allow to cool before serving. Garnish with sliced banana, mango, and toasted sesame seeds. It may be tempting to skip the sesame seeds, but their toasty nutty flavor is integral to this dessert. Definitely worth the extra work.

HAWAIIAN RECIPES

In a tropical paradise like Hawaii, with its plethora of delicious fruits, a smoothie bowl is the ideal breakfast. There are an unlimited number of ways to put one together, but this is my framework recipe for smoothies, and it provides a good balance of fruits, vegetables, fats, and protein. You can make the exact one that I used in the photos, or replace the fruits, juices, and toppings at will. You can drink this smoothie just the way it is out of a glass or put it in a bowl and use it as a canvas for nuts, seeds, granola, and sliced fruit. The choice is yours.

INGREDIENTS:

¼ cup each of three frozen fruits (I used banana, strawberry, and mango)
¼ plain full-fat greek yogurt
¼ cup greens, tightly packed (spinach, kale, etc.)
¼ cup fruit juice (I used pomegranate, but orange is also perfect)
¼ cup ice
1 tbsp nut butter of choice
½ scoop unflavored protein powder (optional)

Toppings: fresh fruit, granola, chia seeds, nuts, goji berries, cacao nibs, whatever you like.

DIRECTIONS:

Put all the ingredients in a blender and puree until smooth. Add water or additional juice if your smoothie is too thick, or a bit more ice or frozen fruit if it is too thin.

Top with additional fresh fruits, granola, seeds, nuts, and whatever else you have around. Not only does it make your smoothie bowl look beautiful, it adds crunch and packs in additional nutrients.

Loco Moco is comfort food at its absolute finest. A hamburger patty on a bed of rice, smothered in gravy, and topped with a fried egg. For me, it screams hangover food (which I think some people call brunch), but it makes a dang good dinner as well. Or, apparently, for teenagers, an afternoon snack. It was first created in the 1940s in Hilo, Hawaii, at a restaurant called the Lincoln Grill as a cheap way to feed a group of local high school athletes called the Lincoln Wreckers. They would come to the restaurant ravenously hungry when they finished their after-school sports, and the owners of the restaurant would sling them an inexpensive and filling plate of hamburger, rice, and brown gravy.

INGREDIENTS:

1 lb. 80/20 ground beef
¼ tsp garlic powder
½ tsp black pepper
Salt, to taste
½ of a sweet onion, finely diced
3 tbsp flour
3 cups beef broth
½ tsp sesame oil
4 cups cooked rice
4 fried eggs
Scallion greens to garnish (optional)

DIRECTIONS:

Add the garlic powder, black pepper, and a good amount of salt to the ground beef and work it into four thin patties.

Heat a large skillet over medium-high heat, and add the hamburger patties. Cook for around 3 minutes on each side, or to your preferred doneness, and then remove them to a plate.

Remove all but 3-4 tbsp of beef fat in the pan. Add the diced onion to the pan and allow it to cook until the edges begin to brown. Add the flour. Stir together and cook until the flour begins to brown.

Add the beef broth ½ cup at a time, stirring each addition until it forms a nice, smooth gravy. This process works better and goes more quickly if the broth is hot. When you have finished adding the broth, you should have a nice, medium-thick gravy. If your gravy is too thick, you can add a bit more broth or water. If it is too thin, you can continue to reduce it until it reaches the desired consistency. When the gravy is finished, remove it from heat and stir in ½ tsp sesame oil.

Serve 1 cup cooked rice topped with a hamburger patty. Smother this with a large scoop of gravy and top with a fried egg. Garnish with scallion greens.

Spam Musubi is one of those dishes that could only come about in Hawaii. It stands as an example of exactly what is so interesting, comforting, and delicious about Hawaiian food. It is based off the Japanese snack onigiri, which are rice balls wrapped in nori and often stuffed with a tasty filling. After WWII, the military stockpiles of spam (and other foods) in Hawaii were made available to the public, and local onigiri makers had a new ingredient to play with.

With a little bit of dressing up, spam musubi becomes something really spectacular. In this recipe I use sushi rice as the base, with its sweet, salty, and sour flavor, and make a soy and brown sugar glaze for the spam. It is only a couple extra steps, and they turn it from a pretty good snack to something worthy of drooling over.

INGREDIENTS:

Sushi Rice:
See recipe on p. 136

Musubi:
1 can spam in 8 slices
1 tbsp + 1 tsp soy sauce
2 tbsp brown sugar
1 tsp rice vinegar
3 sheets of nori

DIRECTIONS:

Slice the spam into eight even, rectangular pieces. Add the spam to a large skillet over medium heat and cook until nicely crisp on both sides.

When all of your spam slices are nicely crisped, remove the pan from heat and allow it to cool for around 1 minute. Add the soy sauce and rice vinegar first, allowing them to absorb some of the heat of the pan, then add the brown sugar. The skillet needs to cool slightly before you do this or you run the risk of immediately turning the sugar into a hard candy. Stir it all around until it forms a nice glaze on the spam, flipping them once to get both sides.

To assemble the spam musubi, begin by slicing the nori sheets into strips around 2 inches wide. Lay down a strip of nori rough side up, and place a slice of spam in the center, perpendicular to the nori. Wet your hands and pick up ~½ cup of the cooked sushi rice. Use your fingers to shape the rice into a rectangular prism of similar size to the spam slice.

Place the rice on top of the slice of spam and wrap the nori around it. Wet your fingers again and seal the nori to itself with a bit of water. Flip the musubi over and voila, there it is.

They're great as an appetizer or a snack, and two can easily be lunch.

Poke has evolved a great deal through time. What began as a quick way to eat freshly caught reef fish, slicing them crosswise and dressing with salt and seaweed, has changed tremendously with the introduction of new flavors to the islands. As immigrants came over from Asia, they brought with them many new ingredients to play with. As with much of Hawaiian food, these new flavors were seamlessly integrated into the local cuisine with delicious results. The recipe below features some of those ingredients and has become of the more popular varieties of poke: ahi shoyu. Made with ahi tuna dressed with soy sauce, sesame oil, and a variety of other flavors, it is a real crowd pleaser.

INGREDIENTS:

Poke:
1 lb. sushi-grade tuna, cut into 1" cubes
¼ cup soy sauce
2 tbsp rice vinegar
2 tsp sesame oil
2 tsp sugar
1 tsp grated ginger
2 scallions, white parts only, sliced thin

Sushi rice:
See recipe on page 136

Accoutrements:
1 cup cucumber, seeded and sliced into ½" cubes
1 cup firm avocado, sliced into ½" cubes
2 scallions, green part only, sliced thinly
2 tbsp toasted sesame seeds
½ cup sriracha mayonnaise (50:50 sriracha:mayo)

DIRECTIONS:

Poke: the poke should be made first and allowed to marinate for 30 minutes to an hour in the refrigerator while you prepare the rest of the meal.

Start by whisking together the soy sauce, sesame oil, vinegar, sugar, ginger, and scallions. Slice your fish into 1" cubes and add to the bowl. Mix it well and place in the fridge to marinate. That's all there is to it.

Sushi rice:
See recipe on page 136

Poke Bowl Assembly:
Divide the rice evenly into 4 bowls, creating a nice layer at the bottom.

Mix the cubed cucumber and avocado into the tuna poke, and divide this evenly atop the bed of sushi rice.

Give the bowls a nice squirt of sriracha mayonnaise and sprinkle over the toasted sesame seeds and scallion greens. And then dig in.

HAWAIIAN MAC SALAD

The plate lunch is as Hawaiian as it gets. You can find them all over the islands, and they always have the same formula: a meat, two scoops of rice, and one scoop of macaroni salad. On my last trip to Hawaii, I tried to sample as many plate lunches as I could find. Fortunately, there are restaurants and food trucks serving them up all over the place. My favorite was found on the road to Hana. This man set up a stand on a pull-out off the road and made an amazing kalua pork and mac salad. The real icing on the cake was that he served the meal on a banana leaf and cut fresh chopsticks for you from bamboo, so it was all garbage-free.

The biggest surprise for me with plate lunches was the mac salad. I knew that the huli huli chicken and kalua pork were going to be amazing, but I was not expecting to fall in love with Hawaiian mac salad the way that I did. I am used to the mediocre stuff that occasionally shows up at potlucks in the contiguous states, and this is certainly not that.

Next time you want to knock some socks off at a barbecue or simply introduce your friends to the beauty of the plate lunch, give this recipe a try. Trust me, it'll be eaten with startling speed.

INGREDIENTS:

1 lb. macaroni
1½ cups grated carrot (about 2 large carrots)
½ cup scallions, white part only (~2 bunches)
1½ cups mayonnaise
2 tbsp apple cider vinegar
2 tsp brown sugar
½ cup whole milk
¼ tsp garlic powder
1 tsp black pepper
Salt, to taste

DIRECTIONS:

Cook and drain the macaroni and put it in a large bowl. Add the grated carrot and scallions.

In a smaller bowl, combine the mayonnaise, milk, vinegar, sugar, garlic powder, and black pepper. Mix well.

Pour the dressing over the macaroni and stir in. Add salt to taste.

Allow to rest in the refrigerator for 1-2 hours for the flavors to combine and mellow.

HULI-HULI CHICKEN

Huli, in Hawaiian, means turn. This dish gets its name from a style of barbecuing chickens on a spit or rotisserie, where they are turned and turned to cook a perfect, juicy, delicious chicken.

It is, essentially, a teriyaki-style marinade, supplemented with Hawaiian flavors. Like many Hawaiian foods, it is rooted in a combination of different cultures and cooking techniques, and is absolutely delicious. The sauce serves as both marinade and basting sauce and is full of that delicious fusion of flavors that make Hawaiian food so good.

INGREDIENTS:

3 lbs. Boneless, skinless chicken thighs
⅓ cup ketchup
½ cup soy sauce
½ cup brown sugar, packed
5 large cloves of garlic, minced
1 thumb-sized piece of ginger, minced/grated
2 tbsp rice vinegar
½ tsp sesame oil
1 large can of pineapple rings (~20 oz.)

DIRECTIONS:

Mix the ketchup, soy sauce, brown sugar, garlic, ginger, vinegar, and sesame oil in a large bowl. Open the can of pineapple and pour the juice in as well. Stir it all up until well-combined.

Reserve about a cup of the sauce for basting. The rest will be the marinade. That way you can baste with the reserved sauce and not need to worry about undercooking it.

Add the chicken thighs to the bowl with the remaining sauce, and put it in the fridge for at least a few hours marinate.

Grill the chicken over a hot grill or in a hot grill pan for 13-15 minutes, flipping several times. Near the end of the cook, baste with the reserved sauce.

While the chicken is resting, grill the pineapple rings to garnish.

CULINARY NIRVANA

Have you ever tried cooking with headphones on? No? Give it a shot. The first time I did it completely changed the way I think about cooking. Up to that point I wasn't conscious of just how engaged all of your senses are in the kitchen. When you think about cooking, there are a few obvious senses that you use often (taste, smell), but the closer you look, the more you realize that the environment of the kitchen is an incredibly rich sensory environment, and that as the cook, you're using all of that information all the time.

The first sense that comes to mind when we think about cooking is almost certainly taste. That's the big one, the no brainer. Cooking is about creating something that tastes amazing, so of course our tongues are the most important instrument in making good food. And the nose is a close second. We've all had the experience of stepping into a room with an empty belly and being carried off into the ether by the scent of frying garlic, and with good reason: our noses are actually even more powerful than our tongues when it comes to taste. While we think of our tongues as the center of flavor perception, they are only taking in the five basics: sweet, sour, salty, bitter, and umami. Everything that you experience beyond that base, all those subtle, complex, amazing flavor combinations, those are actually happening in your nose. Maybe those wine-sniffing sommeliers are onto something after all. But, as a chef, your nose isn't only there to let you appreciate the aroma of that slowly simmering beef bourguignon, it is also constantly supplying information about how the cook is going.

We have all, at one point or another, become aware of a culinary failure by the acrid smell of smoke, whether from a bag of popcorn that spent too long in the microwave, a piece of bread too

close to the broiler, or a forgotten sauce on the back burner, but your nose is more than just a fleshy smoke detector. Next time you're cooking, I challenge you to pay a little bit more attention to the power of the schnozz. You will start to notice that, in addition to letting you know that the popcorn is ruined, your nose can also clue you in to subtler details. You may notice the distinct smell of perfect caramelization on a seared piece of beef, or be able to tell that the edges of the brownie pan have reached that ideal chewiness and need to come out. As you hone this skill, it really does start to feel like a superpower.

Sight is another sense that's easy to understand in the kitchen. Humans are incredibly visual creatures, and sight is undoubtedly our most used sense on a daily basis. The same, of course, is true while cooking. Sure, our senses of taste and smell are more engaged in the kitchen than nearly anywhere else in life, but our actions are still completely reliant on our eyes. Whether it's determining the perfect pinkness of a lamb chop, artfully arranging a beautiful plate, or just grabbing a knife off the table, sight is constantly in use in cooking. There is certainly an artistic eye to perfectly cooked and plated dishes, but I think little of that will come as a surprise to you.

Touch in the kitchen has myriad uses as well, from hovering a hand above a pan to judge its temperature before use to determining the tenderness of a baked potato by gently inserting the tines of a fork, and even giving a cooking protein a quick prod of the finger to guess at its internal temperature. But, most importantly, we use touch when we taste, to make sure that our food has the right balance of textures: not too mushy, not too chewy, not too crunchy.

This is the gorgeous art of mouthfeel, something that we don't talk about much in western cuisine. Texture is important to us, sure, no one likes overcooked vegetables, but we do not have the same appreciation for it that is evident in some Eastern cuisines, where ingredients are often added to a dish specifically for their unique chewiness or sliminess. In western cuisines, that tends to end at crunch. We hate a dish without crunch, but don't have much appreciation for other textures. Perfect dishes are all about balance, and texture is a characteristic that needs to be balanced well. How much better is a bowl of soup with a few croutons or a handful of oyster crackers strewn over the top? Touch may not seem like the most important sense in the kitchen, but it is

engaged just as much as any of the others.

Hearing, though: do we really use our ears when we're cooking and eating? Again, if you haven't ever cooked with headphones on, I encourage you to give it a shot. Cooking and music go together beautifully, we all know that. When you are bouncing around the kitchen from task to task and the music hits right, there's nothing better. But headphones just don't work. I discovered this one day when Ayana was on a work call in the bus. I was starting dinner and wanted to listen to some tunes, so I threw my headphones on and cranked them up. It was all going fine through the prep phase, and then I threw the protein into the pan. I knew that it was hot enough, I'd tested the heat with the back of my hand, but I realized that without hearing that sizzle, I couldn't be certain that things were going to plan. When I took off my headphones it dawned on me just how much information there is coming at you at all times in the kitchen, and how important the proper interpretation of that info is to cooking really well. That sizzle in the pan isn't just a nice sound, it also lets you in on details like your pan temperature and whether your oil is doing what you want it to. Even hearing, the sense we probably all think of as the least important in the kitchen, is constantly feeding us information about how the cook is going.

When you take a step back and think about all of this sensory information together, it's quite a lot. Say you have three dishes going at once, a starch, a protein, and a vegetable, not only will you be watching each of them, tasting when appropriate, and constantly inhaling their aromas as they cook, you are also judging the texture so you can pull them just when they reach the right tenderness, and constantly hearing how everything is hissing, sizzling, and bubbling. The kitchen and the dinner table are the most sensory-rich environments that we experience on a regular basis, and I think that's what makes cooking so magical.

I've spent a lot of my life chasing flow state experiences. When I was younger I mostly found them playing soccer and snowboarding. As I got older, I turned to trail running. It was also part of why I enjoyed wildland firefighting. Each of those activities has the same sort of intense moments, when things are happening all around you, and you need to move quickly, efficiently, and

correctly, that are somehow both frenetic and tranquil. The inner monologue quiets and the decision-making part of the brain goes to autopilot. For a moment you are just a well-oiled machine gliding through a difficult task with grace and ease. It is a moment of pure experience, and there is really nothing else like it. It is what I imagine nirvana to be like, a state of true peace. And, for me at least, the best place to find it is the kitchen.

As a chef, my favorite times are when I am right on the brink of having too much going on. When the kitchen is buzzing, the protein is in the pan, the vegetables need seasoning, the starch is ready to come out, and the sauce is ready to begin. That may not sound like nirvana to you, but it's those moments when you can really lose yourself into that pure, meditative state, where all of your senses are engaged, your mind is quiet, and you just work. Ideally, this is just as that glass of wine hits and your favorite song comes on the speaker, and you can find a little flow to your movements as you stir, strain, spin, slice, and sauce. That's what cooking is all about.

When you're first learning to cook, a lot of that sensory information goes over your head, and, if it doesn't, it can be overwhelming. But the deeper you get into it, the more of it becomes almost instinctual. Little bits of information, like a whiff of the onions just browning, might be superfluous to you at first, you probably won't even notice it, but eventually become a little tap on the shoulder, or a whisper in the ear, letting you know that everything is going to plan. As the dishes progress on the stove, the sensory whispers guide you through a constant flow of tasks: flip this, stir that, chop this, and an instinctual, meditative rhythm takes over. Those are the moments of culinary nirvana.

The recipes in this book constitute a wide range of different ingredients, cuisines, techniques, and complexities. For the novice cook they are not necessarily what I would call easy. As you try these dishes, I encourage you to push yourself a little bit. Challenge yourself and to pay attention to all of that sensory information you're receiving. There's a lot of good stuff in there.

JAPANESE RECIPES

Yakitori, literally "grilled bird," is a dish of grilled chicken, and is serious business in Japan. Like other culinary specialties in Japan (think sushi, tempura, ramen), there are many restaurants that serve only yakitori. These yakitori joints are hyper-specialized, serving up every part of the chicken, but always grilled, typically skewered, and only seasoned in one of two ways: salt and pepper, or with a lacquer-like tare glaze. And usually alongside a few cold beers.

The recipe below is for a traditional momo yakitori, which is made with just boneless, skinless chicken thighs glazed with a tare sauce. If you want to spice things up, negima is a common variation, where scallions or pieces of leek are put between the chunks of chicken thigh. And, if you're feeling a bit more adventurous, you can try removing the skin yourself, skewering it up, and making torikawa, skewers of just grilled chicken skin.

INGREDIENTS:

1½ lbs. boneless, skinless chicken thighs
½ cup soy sauce
½ cup mirin
¼ cup sake
¼ cup water
1 tbsp brown sugar
1 tbsp minced garlic
1 tbsp minced ginger

DIRECTIONS:

Combine all ingredients except chicken in a saucepan and bring to a boil. Reduce heat and simmer for 20 minutes to reduce the sauce. Once nicely reduced, allow it to cool and set aside ¼ cup for the final baste.

Slice chicken thighs into 1" cubes and marinate for 30 minutes in the larger portion of the sauce. Soak the bamboo skewers in water during this time.

Fill the skewers with chicken pieces and cook on a medium-high heat grill or grill pan until cooked through, ~3 minutes on each side. Baste with the marinade while cooking.

When each skewer is cooked through, remove it to a plate to rest. Before serving, baste each skewer with the reserved sauce and sprinkle with toasted sesame seeds and finely chopped scallion greens.

SESAME SOBA

Soba are a Japanese noodle made primarily from buckwheat flour. In parts of Japan, soba is the primary starch, and people often eat them several times a day. The noodles are nutty, slightly bitter, and delicious eaten both in hot soups and cold salads. The recipe that I've prepared here is a cold salad of soba noodles dressed with soy sauce and sesame oil, and tossed with cucumbers and scallions. It is the kind of meal that you can throw together in ten minutes and you will be happy to eat every night of the week.

Like many foods that are now distinctly Japanese, soba noodles originally arrived from China. They are made primarily from buckwheat flour, which gave them some distinct advantages historically. Firstly, buckwheat has higher levels of protein and fiber than wheat, as well as being naturally gluten-free. Secondly, and historically more importantly, buckwheat is also high in thiamine, a nutrient which is very low in white rice. A dietary deficiency of thiamine leads to a condition called beriberi, which is quite debilitating. Perhaps counterintuitively, in Japan during the Edo period the wealthy residents of what is now Tokyo were more susceptible to thiamine deficiency due to their high consumption of more expensive white rice, while the rural poor, who ate a diet high in soba, were unlikely to develop beriberi. Eventually, the pieces of that puzzle were all put together, and the people of Tokyo began eating large quantities of soba as well, a tradition that exists to this day.

INGREDIENTS:

8 oz. soba noodles
⅓ cup soy sauce
2 tbsp rice vinegar
2 tbsp sesame oil
½ tsp black pepper
2 tsp sugar
½ cup scallions, thinly slices
1 tbsp toasted sesame seeds
½ cucumber, peeled and thinly sliced

DIRECTIONS:

Start the noodles in a pot of lightly salted water and boil around 8-10 minutes until cooked.

While the noodles are boiling, combine soy sauce, rice vinegar, sesame oil, pepper, and sugar in a mixing bowl and stir until the sugar dissolves. Use a bowl large enough for the noodles as well.

When the noodles are finished, drain them and add them to the bowl with the sauce. Add the cucumber, scallion, and sesame seeds as well. Toss until everything is well-coated in sauce and serve.

Garnish with additional sliced scallions and toasted sesame seeds, if desired. Serves two.

Ahh, tempura, a dish that is somehow both deep-fried and light. It brings all of the joys of fried food without leaving one feeling like they need a nap afterward. How does one create such perfection? That light, amazing fry is achieved using a batter made from egg, wheat flour, and ice cold water. Sometimes baking soda is used to lighten the batter, and carbonated water can be used as well. When going for maximum crispiness and lightness, I like to use a bit of both.

INGREDIENTS:

Batter:
1 egg + cold seltzer to equal 1 cup
1 cup flour
¼ tsp salt
½ tsp baking soda

Other:
Vegetable oil (or other high-heat oil)
Whatever you'd like to fry (our favorites below)
Shrimp
Sweet Potatoes
Broccoli
Apple Slices
Green Beans
Onion Slices

Dipping Sauces:
Ponzu
Sriracha Mayo (50:50 sriracha:mayo)

DIRECTIONS:

Before you start anything else, get everything you want to fry chopped and placed. This is a fast-paced meal once you start going, so you don't want to be distracted trying to chop broccoli at the same time that you are manning the fryer.

Once all your ingredients are chopped and ready, beat one egg in a measuring cup and add ice cold seltzer water to a total of 1 cup. Add this to a bowl. In a separate measuring cup, add 1 cup flour, ½ tsp baking soda, and ¼ tsp salt. Mix these dry ingredients and then add them to the bowl with the egg and seltzer. Mix this sparingly with chopsticks. It is totally okay for there to be big bunches of flour in the batter—in fact, this is a good sign that you did not overmix it. Mixing the batter creates gluten, which makes the batter heavy, and undoes that beautiful, light, crunchy tempura texture.

Heat your oil in a saucepan or wok to 340-360 degrees. Dredge the food item in flour and then dip it in your tempura batter, trying to get a light, even coating. Drop into the oil. Try to fill the wok without overcrowding it or cooling the oil too much. Each time you add something to the oil, it reduces the temperature slightly, so do your best to keep an eye on the temperature. If it gets too low, let it heat up again before you add any additional items. Frying at too low a temperature leads to a soggy, oily finished product.

Tempura also has a tendency to lose its crunch quickly after cooking, so this meal is best done as you go, with people eating each batch while it is still hot and crisp.

SUSHI RICE

Sushi can be really pretentious. And that pretension is often what makes cooking a dish for the first time intimidating. But it doesn't need to be that way. Sure, really good sushi is really good. But, it turns out, even the poorly-wrapped, wonky rolls are still really good. And the origins of sushi are actually pretty simple. The word sushi means sour-tasting, and refers to the vinegared rice which is used, but sushi actually originates from narezushi, an ancient Chinese method of preserving fish in fermented rice. Old fish wrapped in moldy rice. See? Not so pretentious there.

Sushi rice serves as a base for a few dishes in this cookbook. The sweet, sour, salty, sticky stuff is not only great rolled up in nori and topped with fish, it is also the delicious platform for spam musubi and makes a great base for a poke bowl.

INGREDIENTS:

2 cups short or medium grain japanese rice
2 cups water
½ cup rice vinegar
1 tbsp sugar
1 tsp salt

DIRECTIONS:

On the stove, combine 2 cups of short-grain sushi rice and 2 cups of water in a pot over medium-high heat. Cover and bring to a boil.

When it reaches a boil, reduce the heat to low and allow it to simmer for 10 minutes. Uncover it as infrequently as possible. If necessary, you may lift the lid briefly to peek in or to let off a little bit of excess heat, but try to keep it covered the entire time, relying on sound to tell you how it is doing.

After the rice has simmered for 10 minutes, remove it from heat and allow it to steam for another 10 minutes. Do not uncover it during this time, the steaming is very important.

After 10 minutes have passed, your rice should be perfectly al dente. At this point, mix together the rice vinegar, sugar, and salt in a large bowl until the sugar and salt have dissolved. Add the rice to the bowl and stir it well to combine. Then allow it to cool so that you can easily handle it.

BUSLIFE SUSHI FOUR WAYS

The one big trouble with making sushi while traveling the back roads and hinterlands of this country is sourcing high-quality fish. Out there, in the middle of the desert, one is unlikely to stumble upon a fish monger with fine cuts of sushi-grade tuna. But fear not, fellow vehicle-dwellers, there are plenty of delicious sushi rolls that can be made with products available in nearly every grocery store in the country. Below you will find four of our favorite buslife-ready, camping-approved, desert-capable sushi recipes.

INGREDIENTS:

Sushi Rice:
See Recipe on p.136

1 package nori (10 sheets)

Fillings:
¼ lb. large raw shrimp
¼ lb. imitation crab leg
3 oz. smoked salmon
4 oz. cream cheese
2 avocados, sliced ¼" lengthwise
2 cucumbers, peeled and sliced into long matchsticks
1 bunch scallions
bamboo sushi mat (optional)

DIRECTIONS:

Begin by laying out one sheet of nori, rough side up. Scoop on enough rice to cover the middle two thirds of the sheet (lengthwise), but only about 2 grains deep. You want good coverage with a nice, thin layer of rice, and a bit of uncovered nori on either side.

In the center of your rice, place a small portion of your fillings. It is easy to overfill, so try to just put 1 small piece of each filling in any area, running the length of the sheet of nori.

When you have your fillings all laid out, pick up one side of the nori and roll it about halfway to compact the ingredients. Then set it back down, pick up the other side, and roll it the entire way, taking time to compact things and get a tight roll as you go.

When you get to the end, dip your fingers in a bit of water and run it along the last bit of nori to wet it and form a seal. Place the rolled sushi seam side down for the best seal. Slice each roll into 6-8 even pieces and serve with soy sauce, wasabi, and pickled ginger.

California Roll: imitation crab leg, cucumber, avocado
Philadelphia Roll: smoked salmon, cream cheese, cucumber
Shrimp Tempura Roll: shrimp tempura, cucumber, avocado
Scallion Tempura Roll: scallion tempura, cucumber, avocado
(for tempura, see recipe on p.135)

FURUTSU SANDO

Something like a strawberry shortcake, furutsu sando is a sandwich made with whipped cream, whatever fruits are in season, and, traditionally, Japanese milk bread. It is light, delicate, and delicious. And when properly prepared, it can be quite stunning on the plate. While technically these sandwiches should be made with milk bread, any firm white bread will do just fine. I typically look for something in the "farm-house" style, as that usually means it is a little bit heartier.

INGREDIENTS:

1 cup heavy whipping cream
2 tsp powdered sugar
¼ tsp vanilla extract
6 slices firm white bread
1 kiwi
1 orange
6 strawberries

DIRECTIONS:

Add the cream, sugar, and vanilla to a mixing bowl and whisk until the whipped cream is nice and thick, and holds a peak.

Prepare your fruit by peeling skins, trimming tops, and slicing into neat pieces to put in the sandwich and create a beautiful cross-section when the sandwich is sliced.

Place a slice of bread on a piece of cling wrap and cover the bread with a healthy scoop of whipped cream. Position your fruits carefully to ensure good coverage and a beautiful finished product. A line of fruit down the center that will be perfectly bisected when cut is key. Cover the fruits with more whipped cream and a second slice of bread. Wrap tightly, and place it in the refrigerator.

When all the sandwiches are in the refrigerator or freezer, lay a baking tray over them and add a small amount of weight to compress them. Keep them in the fridge for several hours to allow them to set and stiffen.

After the sandwiches have cooled for several hours, remove them from the fridge. Carefully unwrap and slice them, first removing the crust and then slicing diagonally to create the beautiful fruit cross-sections. Be sure to wipe the blade of your knife between each cut to clean off any whipped cream, which would mar the look of the finished product.

TEX-MEX RECIPES

SALSA BLANCA

In southeastern Virginia, where I grew up, Salsa Blanca is a staple at every Mexican restaurant. When you sit down, someone hustles over with a basket of chips accompanied by the traditional salsa roja and this delicious, mysterious stuff. In the seven cities area, you cannot run a successful Mexican restaurant without it—people just won't come. It wasn't until I first moved out of Virginia that I realized no one else in the world eats it (or has ever heard of it).

It turns out this sauce was invented at a Mexican restaurant called El Toro in Norfolk, Virginia in the 1960s. It was originally created as a salad dressing, and customer innovation led to it slowly migrating its way from the salad bar to the table as a second dip for tortilla chips. The original recipe was a closely guarded secret, but there are a few people out there who claim to have some inside knowledge. Below you will find my attempt at reverse-engineering the recipe, which I think is pretty darn accurate.

It is no easy feat to figure out a recipe based on taste memories of something that you haven't had in years, but I think this one is authentic. At the very least, it both transports me back to the favorite restaurant of my childhood and passes the general audience test as being damn delicious.

It is an easy salsa to throw together next time you're having tacos, and I promise it won't disappoint. It ain't real classy, but it is undoubtedly delicious. And if you're ever in the Hampton Roads area, stop in at Plaza Azteca (the Mexican restaurant of my youth) and get yourself some of the good stuff.

INGREDIENTS:

2 cups mayonnaise (I like Helmann's or Duke's)
½ cup milk
1 tsp crushed red pepper
1 ½ tsp dried oregano
1 ½ tsp garlic powder
1 tsp cumin
¼ cup pickled jalapeno brine
1 tsp agave nectar or honey

DIRECTIONS:

This one is pretty simple—the only trick is that you can't eat it right away. Mix everything together and pop it in the fridge. It is one of those things that gets better with time, so you can eat it after a few hours, but the next day is better, and some purists say it needs a minimum or two days to mature properly.

Serve it with some nice tortilla chips and preferably alongside a nice salsa roja (see p.20) to get the full experience. I was never a double-dipper, but some folks insist that you should have both salsa blanca and salsa roja on every chip.

15-MINUTE BLACK BEAN SOUP

When it comes to the equation of time put into a meal versus enjoyment derived from the product, I think that this may be the finest recipe I have ever created. You can throw this soup together in what feels like no time, and it is both healthy and absolutely delicious. If you have an immersion blender, this soup will immediately become a staple in your kitchen. If you don't have one, check out the recommendations at thebuslifekitchen.com, because you want one.

This soup is a perfect meal for a chilly fall evening when you are tired from working, a cold winter's night when you are worn down by the long dark, or a beautiful spring or summer day, when you want something simple and quick so that you can spend as much time as possible enjoying the weather. It is somehow both light and hearty while also being creamier than it deserves to be with that ingredient list. Make it this week—tonight even—you won't regret it.

INGREDIENTS:

2 cans black beans
1 medium onion, yellow or white
1 jalapeno
3 cloves garlic
1 tbsp cumin
2 cups vegetable broth
Cilantro and sour cream to garnish

DIRECTIONS:

Chop your onion, garlic, and jalapeno roughly and toss into a hot pot with an ample amount of oil and the cumin. Cook over medium-high heat, stirring occasionally, until the edges of the onions are slightly burnt.

Dump the two cans of black beans into the pot, liquid and all. Stir this up and then add the broth. Scrape the bottom to make sure you pick up any fond present. Simmer this for a couple minutes and then turn off the heat.

Use your immersion blender to puree the soup to a fine texture.

Salt to taste. Top with chopped cilantro and sour cream. A few crushed tortilla chips on top wouldn't be bad either.

GREEN CHILE CHEESE DIP

This green chile dip is the kind of appetizer that you can throw together in 5 minutes and people will rave about through the entire party—until it's gone, at least. It is perfect as a game day snack or as part of a spread of nibbles for your guests. There's nothing fancy about it, but it is dang good.

The delicate flavors of fire-roasted green chiles and spices permeate the gooey cheese, creating something undeniably good. Serve it with tortilla chips or vegetables... heck, it'd probably be good on old shoe leather.

INGREDIENTS:

8 oz. cream cheese
1 cup sharp cheddar cheese
1 cup roasted green chiles
1 tsp cumin
1 tsp chili powder
½ cup bell pepper, minced (red, green, or both ideally)
¼ cup milk

DIRECTIONS:

Mix ingredients well and cook over low heat, stirring regularly, until melted together.

Serve with sliced peppers, carrots, celery, or tortilla chips.

While I was perfecting my arroz con leche (recipe on p.26) and eating it nearly every day, it struck me that I ought to try using the same technique in a savory context. Here that same silkiness of a rice pudding is infused with broth, spices, and a bit of cheese, creating a really excellent side dish or starch on which to rest a beautiful protein. My favorite way to eat this dish, which I am calling Tex-Mex risotto, is with some charred peppers and onions and a thinly sliced grilled or seared piece of chicken.

INGREDIENTS:

1 cup rice
1 cup water
2 cups milk
2 cups vegetable broth
2 roasted poblanos, peeled and diced
½ tsp cumin
½ tsp chili powder
½ tsp garlic powder
4 oz. sharp cheddar, grated
2 tbsp lime juice
1 can black beans (optional)
salt, to taste

DIRECTIONS:

Put rice in a large pot and add roughly 1 cup water, just enough to barely cover the rice. Turn heat to medium-high and cook until the water is nearly absorbed, stirring regularly to keep the rice from sticking to the bottom.

Reduce heat to medium and add the diced poblanos and spices. Then begin adding the broth ½ cup at a time. Cook until the liquid is mostly absorbed and then add the next ½ cup. Continue to stir regularly and scrape the bottom through these additions, as the rice will stick.

When the broth is done, continue the process with the milk, adding it in ½ cup increments and stirring and scraping regularly. After the last of the milk has been added, cook until it is largely absorbed and try your rice. It should be nicely cooked, perhaps slightly al dente. If it is not yet cooked to your liking, add a touch more broth and cook until it reaches your desired consistency.

When the rice is perfect, remove the pot from heat and add in your grated cheese and lime juice. Stir to allow the cheese to melt and mix in. Add salt to taste.

If you are eating this as a standalone dish, you can mix in a can of black beans and enjoy a bowl just like that or use it as a base for charred onions and bell peppers and grilled chicken or beef.

RESTAURANT-STYLE QUESO DIP

The trick to a good queso dip is mostly in the cheese. You need a cheese with a high fat content and low melting point, so that it will dissolve into that creamy, silky texture, and stay liquid for as long as possible. The trick that works best (and that most restaurants use) is american cheese. It turns out that the best queso dip is actually incredibly easy to make. Just melt some american cheese with milk, green chile, and spices, and voila, beautiful queso dip.

While I know that none of us like to think that the delicious queso dip from our favorite Mexican restaurant is actually just american cheese, it probably is. At best there's a bit of monterey jack mixed in there as well. Queso dip is a very much a Tex-Mex thing, and american cheese is the best tool for the job. So, belly up to the deli counter (the easiest place to find it), get yourself a pound of white american cheese, and give it a shot. I promise it's delicious.

INGREDIENTS:

1 pound white american cheese
½ cup whole milk
1 cup green chiles
½ tsp garlic powder
½ tsp cumin

DIRECTIONS:

Melt the cheese with milk over medium-low heat. Stir in the green chile and spices. Stir to incorporate. Serve in a warmed bowl to keep the consistency longer.

Serve with plenty of tortilla chips, it'll go fast.

STOVETOP CHICKEN NACHOS

Growing up, chicken nachos were my absolute favorite food. There was a Mexican restaurant close to my house, and my friend and I would walk over there after school to gorge on glorious plates of chips, chicken, and cheese. The trick to their nachos, which puts them on a tier above every other nacho plate I've had, is the use of queso. Melted cheese is wonderful, but by pouring queso over the top first they ensure that cheese reaches every chips, eliminating for good the dreaded under-topped nacho.

I spent years reverse-engineering their recipe, with the queso being the most difficult aspect to replicate. I tried many variations to reproduce that perfect queso, everything from the simple velveeta and rotel recipe all the way to a modified mornay sauce. But, as is often the case, one of the simplest turns out to be the best. In the bus, we forego the melted cheese and just pile up some chips with shredded chicken and queso dip, then load it up with all the fixings. Give it a shot and see what you've been missing.

INGREDIENTS:

Shredded Chicken:
1 lb. chicken breast
½ yellow onion, sliced thin
4 cloves garlic
2 tbsp tomato paste
1 cup chicken broth
Juice of 1 lime
1 tsp cumin
1 tsp chili powder
Salt to taste

Toppings:
Tortilla Chips
Queso (see recipe on p.144)
Enchilada Sauce/Salsa Roja
Shredded Iceberg Lettuce
Mexican Sour Cream
Sliced Black Olives
Pico de Gallo

DIRECTIONS:

Shredded Chicken:
Sear the chicken in a saucepan over medium-high heat to achieve a nice brown crust on both sides. Add onions and garlic and cook until onions are browning at edges. Add tomato paste and cook for a minute or two until slightly darkened. Add broth, lime, and spices, reduce heat to medium-low, and simmer, stirring occasionally, until chicken can be easily shredded with a fork. Remove from heat and adjust seasoning with salt. Allow to cool until you can touch it easily. Shred the chicken with two forks and return it to the pan, mixing it with the onions and sauce.

Queso Dip:
See Recipe on p.144

Nachos:
Lay out a layer of tortilla chips, pour over a nice helping of queso dip, add a handful of shredded chicken, and cover the lot with your choice of toppings. I would suggest iceberg lettuce, sliced black olives, pico de gallo, and a drizzle of sour cream and enchilada sauce (p.24) or salsa roja (p.20).

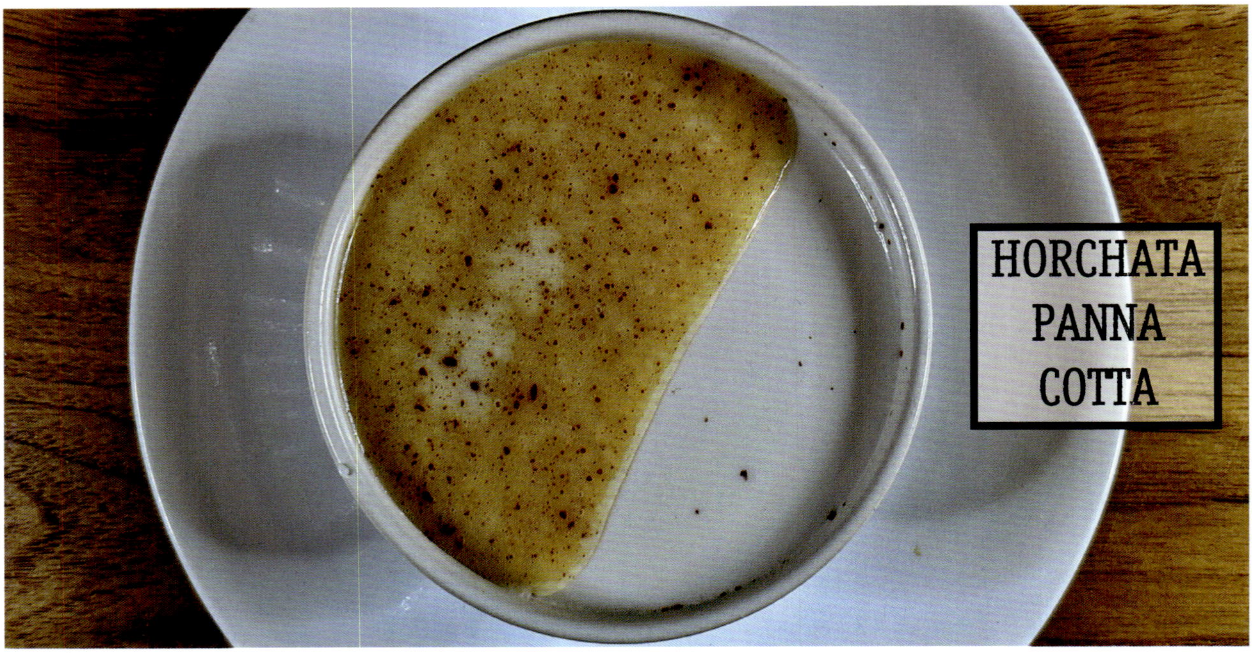

HORCHATA PANNA COTTA

For me, an ice cold glass of horchata is usually plenty for dessert. On a hot night, after a meal of spicy tacos, it is perfect: light, sweet, and delicious. But, if you want to class things up a bit, panna cotta is an easy way to turn that delicious drink into an elegant dessert. All it takes is the addition of some gelatin. Drizzle over a little bit of sauce made with cinnamon and condensed milk, and you have something truly special.

INGREDIENTS:

Horchata:
4 cups water
1 cup long grain rice
¼ cup sugar
1 large cinnamon stick
1½ cups half & half
¼ tsp vanilla extract

Panna Cotta:
¼ oz. gelatin
(1 envelope)
2 cups horchata

Sauce:
¼ cup condensed milk
⅛ tsp ground cinnamon
½ tbsp butter
1 tbsp milk

DIRECTIONS:

Horchata:
Make the horchata first. Add the rice, water, sugar, and cinnamon stick to a pitcher, stir, and place in the refrigerator for 24 hours. Once 24 hours have passed, blend the mixture well and strain through a sieve. Discard the strained rice bits. Add the half & half and vanilla extract, and stir together.

Panna Cotta:
Put ½ cup cold horchata in a bowl and pour over the envelope of gelatin. Allow the gelatin powder to hydrate for around 5 minutes.

In a saucepan, heat the rest of the horchata over medium-low heat. When the gelatin is hydrated, add that mixture to the saucepan. Heat the horchata until it is warm and the gelatin is fully dissolved. Do not boil.

Pour the horchata from the saucepan into your serving dishes (or molds, if you are feeling bold) and place these in the refrigerator to set for at least 4 hours.

Sauce:
Add the butter, condensed milk, and ground cinnamon to a skillet over low heat. Allow the butter to melt and stir the mixture until well-combined. Add the milk to thin the sauce, toss in a pinch of salt, and remove from heat.

Serving:
Drizzle a bit of the sauce over each panna cotta and enjoy!

MISCELLANEOUS RECIPES

COMPOUND BUTTER

Compound butters are one of the simplest things to make that add the most flourish to a dish. They are made by softening butter, mixing it with flavoring ingredients, and then rolling it in wax paper and resolidifying it in the fridge. The world of compound butters is so open to exploration. There are infinite flavor combinations that can enhance a butter and provide an elegant finish to your dish. Below you will find three of my favorite recipes, but I encourage you to explore your creative side here as well.

INGREDIENTS:

Mint and Garlic:
¼ lb. salted butter
4 cloves garlic, minced
2 tbsp mint, minced
Juice of ½ lime

East Coast Shrimp Butter:
¼ lb. salted butter
¼ cup peeled and cooked shrimp, minced
½ tsp old bay seasoning

Lemon Pepper Shrimp Butter:
¼ lb. salted butter
¼ cup peeled and cooked shrimp, minced
2 tbsp lemon juice
1 tsp fresh black pepper
2 cloves garlic, minced

DIRECTIONS:

The basics of compound butters are all the same, so I will only write them once. Under the ingredients you will find three recipes for compound butters.

Soften the butter on the counter until it is quite soft, a few hours at least (depending on room temperature)

Mince the flavoring ingredients (herbs, garlic, shrimp, etc.) finely, and mix in thoroughly. Add any citrus juice or vinegar, and stir until well-combined.

Spoon the mixture onto a piece of wax paper. Use the wax paper to shape it into a log, and roll it up. Secure the ends with tape or a rubber band. Place this roll back in the fridge to resolidify.

Serve over vegetables, to finish a piece of meat, or simply as an appetizer with a loaf of crusty bread.

STOVE-ROASTED TURKEY

Thanksgiving can be lot of cooking to be done in a tiny kitchen, and it's made doubly hard for those of us who chose not to put ovens in our builds. Fortunately, this recipe provides a solution, making a true Thanksgiving feast possible in your rig, even if, like us, you only have a stove. This recipe is not exactly the baked turkey that you've had in the past, but the use of wine and broth in a closed pan creates a juicy and incredibly tender turkey that will delight your guests.

INGREDIENTS:

5 lb. turkey breast
¼ cup minced poultry herbs (rosemary, sage, thyme)
1 onion, diced
2 carrots, diced
2 celery ribs, diced
3 cloves garlic, minced
2 cups dry white wine
2 cups light broth (chicken or turkey)
Olive oil
Salt + Pepper

DIRECTIONS:

Begin by spatchcocking the turkey breast. This method allows better heat transfer through the breast. To spatchcock the breast, cut down either side of the spine all the way until it can be removed. Next, spread the back as wide as you can and apply pressure to the center of the breast until it pops and lays flat.

Pat the turkey breast dry and then coat all over with olive oil, salt, pepper, and minced poultry herbs.

Heat the large, heavy-bottomed pan over medium-high heat and add a fair amount of olive oil to the pan. When it gets nice and hot, add the bird, breast down. Sear the skin until nicely browned all around. Remove the bird from the pan.

Add another bit of olive oil and the onion, garlic, celery, and carrots to the pot. Cook, stirring regularly, until the onions are translucent. At this point, put the turkey breast into the pot on a roasting rack above the vegetables, skin up, and add ½ cup each of broth and white wine. Cover, reduce the heat to low, and allow to simmer.

The turkey breast should take around 15 minutes per pound. Check occasionally to ensure that there is always plenty of liquid in there. Add broth and wine in equal measure as needed. Cook the bird to an internal temperature of 165 degrees. When done, remove the turkey and allow it to rest for 5-10 minutes, and turn off the heat. The remaining vegetables and liquid in the bottom of the pot can be pureed to serve as a sauce.

If you are looking for a Thanksgiving dessert that will absolutely knock the family's socks off, this pumpkin creme brulee is the dish. Falling neatly in the middle between rustic family feast and haute cuisine, this dish is both familiar and elegant, featuring all your favorite flavors and textures of both creme brulee and pumpkin pie, and is certain to delight any and all of your Thanksgiving guests.

INGREDIENTS:

- 2 cups heavy cream
- 2 tsp pumpkin pie spice
- 2 tbsp brown sugar
- 6 large egg yolks
- ⅓ cup white sugar
- 1 tsp vanilla
- ½ cup pumpkin puree

DIRECTIONS:

Whisk together egg yolks, white sugar, and vanilla in a mixing bowl and set aside. You will need to use a double boiler later, so it is good to mix these ingredients in a vessel that can be used for that.

Add the cream, pumpkin pie spice, and brown sugar to a smaller pot on the stove over medium heat. Stir to combine well and allow the brown sugar to dissolve into the cream. Scald the cream, stirring often while bringing it to just before boiling. There should be bubbles around the edge, but not a proper boil. When you reach this state, remove it from heat.

Pour the cream in a small stream into the egg mixture while whisking. The small stream is important to keep the eggs from cooking on contact. When all the cream is added to the eggs, add the pumpkin puree and whisk to combine well.

Heat the mixture over a double boiler, stirring often, until it thickens. You can eyeball it based on how well it coats the back of a spoon, but I would suggest using a thermometer. The custard will begin to set at around 160 degrees. You do not want to heat it beyond 185. 175-180 is your sweet spot. The custard will have variable temperatures throughout, so stir well and often, and gauge the temperature at different places in the pot.

Once the custard has been brought to temperature, remove it from heat and divide it into four 5 oz. ramekins. Put the ramekins in the refrigerator for at least 1 hour to set. You can also make this in the morning or even a day or two ahead, just be sure to cover the ramekins so that they do not form a skin on the top of the custard.

When you are ready to serve, spread ½ tbsp sugar evenly on the top of each ramekin, and hit it with a blowtorch to create the sugar shell. This can alternatively be done under the broiler, but if you do it that way, you may overheat the custard and need to return the ramekins to the fridge and allow them to set again.

CONCLUSION

Many times through the course of producing this book, through the years of work amidst a global pandemic and an ever-worsening climate crisis, I've stopped and asked myself: "is any of this worthwhile? Is another cookbook really what the world needs right now?" Having spent a lot of time reflecting on these questions, I can say resoundingly that the answer is no. The world needs healing in ten thousand forms, and I wish that I could give them. Unfortunately, I don't have that power alone. But I do think that there are a couple of good pieces in this book—a few things that will hopefully push the needle a notch toward goodness.

For my generation, it can be hard to believe in anything. We came of age into a dying world that refuses to admit that it's sick. Our nation has been in decline since I was old enough to notice, and the rate at which things have gotten worse and less equal has only grown more rapid. The politics in this country have driven a wedge between people, even within families, and we are angrier and more fragmented than we've ever been. It's hard to dream anymore in a world that appears to be on such a bleak path. But, of course, that is not all that there is. The world on the television screen (or that little one in your pocket) is not the same as the world out the window, as much as those blathering idiots on the talk shows might insist that it is. The world out the window will always be a little bit better, if only because you are free to perceive it with your own eyes.

The trouble with this time right now is that nearly everything needs to change. We all need to believe in a future and fight for the dreams and the change that we want to see, and we need to do it together. Despite the violent verb used in the previous sentence, that "fight" is, more often than not, one of kindness.

Food has always been a tool to bring disparate groups together. From our ancient nomadic

ancestors to the present, sharing a meal is one of the most basic forms of altruism that exists. Whether it was inviting your tribe to feast after a large animal was taken on a hunt, or getting to know the strange culture of your new neighbors by sitting down to an unfamiliar dinner, food has a way of transcending our differences and bringing us together over one of our most basic functions.

All of us eat. Most of us, who are lucky enough to have the means, do so two or three (or more) times a day. Tastes may differ slightly among us, but each day we fill our bellies with food, and unlike the other arts, we mostly all like the same things. Few people in this world turn their nose up at a scoop of ice cream, a slice of pizza, or a piece of grilled meat. Some tastes, some experiences, are universal.

This book, like the bus, is a realization of a dream. I do not claim that either of them are doing any real good in the world, but I do hope that they are at least asking people to think. In this book I've tried to open the door to getting to know some other cultures through food. It is often the case, in my experience, that curiosity follows taste. The first visit to a restaurant may simply be to experience a new cuisine, but by the third or fourth, the mind starts to wonder about the people who first developed these foods, what their country looks like, what they do for fun, what they find beautiful. And nothing creates a better world than understanding other people, because we are all the same. As with our taste in food, our life desires differ somewhat from person to person, but we are all driven by very similar wants and needs. And, perhaps most importantly, we are all deserving of the same respect, dignity, and quality of life.

I hope that in exploring these recipes you learn about or are made curious about other people and other cultures, whether the cause is a dish made with Sichuan peppercorns, or just my Indianan grandma's impossible pie. Beyond that, I wish that this book and these recipes will serve as an invitation to create the small-scale connection that we could all use more of in our lives these days. There are, in my experience, few better ways to make a connection than to share a meal with a person. So, cook a meal, invite your friends, your family, and maybe even the new neighbor or coworker that you don't know very well to share in that most ancient and primal act of altruism, eating together. In the end, all we have is each other, and we need to work, love, dream, and, yes, eat together if we're going to survive on this planet.

Whoa, a moral mission at the end of a cookbook?! I didn't see it coming either! But there it is, a task set out for you by me, and one that I know I need to improve on as well. I am delinquent in this duty as much as anyone else. So, if you see us out there on the road, flag us down and say hello, because we'd love to share our table with you.

Thank you again, reader, for picking up this book, and especially for making it all the way to the end. This is the culmination of both a dream and years of hard work, and it really does mean the world to me that you're reading it. I hope that you enjoy all of these recipes and I look forward to sharing many more with you on my website and in future books. Thank you for giving me a reason to keep doing what I love.

Happy eating! Enjoy!

ACKNOWLEDGEMENTS

There are so, so many people that I could and should thank, and I am sure that I will forget many, but here are some people to whom I would like to offer enormous thanks:

Ayana: for your endless love and for always supporting and believing in me (and the countless dishes you washed to make this book possible). I could not have done any of it without you.

Mom: for teaching me to follow my dreams and always, always supporting them.

Dad: for convincing me to eat all those things I hated as a kid, and for all the doors you opened for me.

My Brothers: for showing me that all men ought to cook well.

Dan: for always being a good friend, confidant, and sounding board, even if it does sometimes take us half a dozen whiskeys before we get to the meat of it.

Jon: for being a shining example of someone who focuses his energy on the things that he loves. As Lao Tzu said, “The snow goose need not bathe to make itself white. Neither need you do anything but be yourself.”

Nathan: for being an excellent big brother, always teaching me new things, and always letting your kid brother come along.

Gillian: for being an excellent partner to my brother and mother to your beautiful girls. And also for letting us crash in your basement every xmas.

Brenda: for always having room for us in your house, your yard, your kitchen, and your heart.

Scott and Connie: for welcoming me into the Otteman clan with open arms.

Alan and Shellene: for pushing us over the line to print this book, and for the many shared nights of good food, drink, and cheer (and those to come!)

Aaron: for lifelong friendship and generosity, from the days of LANs to now. And also for keeping my freezer full of ducks.

Ray: for always being a good friend willing to listen to what’s bothering me or just do a few whiskey mysteries and get weird.

Jacky and Trevor: for being my tallest and shortest friends (is that true? definitely not). But seriously, thank you two for always being wonderful friends and for many good nights spent in the dart cave.

JD: for keeping me locked in the basement, forcing me to dream of a life on the road. And also for being one third of JDAndy, a place and group of friends that changed my life.

Cat and Aaron: for showing us the way when we were brand new to buslife.

Amy: for always being such a great example of strength, vulnerability, and creative expression.

Rich and Gia: for giving all of us a reason to travel to Florida, and for being great friends to us and our family (and all the cookies).

Michael Head: for going and studying to be a doctor during a pandemic, and for your advice and encouragement on the kickstarter.

Ruthann and Greg: I'm so excited to be a part of your family. Thank you for the warm welcome in the northwest, and I look forward to getting to know you better.

Lizzy: for always being someone easy to talk to, especially when there are an overwhelming number of new Ottemans to meet.

Ian Bouchard: for being one of the very first people who made me feel like what I was doing might be worth a damn.

Jenny McMurray: your enthusiasm and support has often been a light when I find myself in dark places.

Brock Butterfield: for your generosity toward this project and your role in making #buslife a thing.

Philippe of Our Numinous Nature: for the gorgeous cover art.

Mike of Satsang Vanworks: for sharing the knowledge and picking up our slack when we got in too deep.

To all the hands that aided in the building of our bus, but particularly Zach, Elfie, and Gower, for sharing your labor, tools, and knowledge.

To every follower, subscriber, backer, and reader: none of this would exist without you. Thank you for giving me a chance to keep doing what I love.

INDEX

ABOUT THE AUTHOR

A. J. Forget is a chef, writer, photographer, traveler, and self-proclaimed dilettante. He left a career as a wildland firefighter to pursue his lifelong passion of writing and his outlandish goal of a modern nomadic life. He lives in a converted school bus with his partner, a silversmith and dream-worker, and their eternally-sleepy dog, traveling the world in pursuit of natural beauty, grand adventure, and the tastiest food out there.